Tale of the *Green Dragon*

Copyright © 2011 by James H. Irwin, Jr.

Front cover photograph "*Green Dragon*" by Larry LeGault. Mr. Legault's work includes landscapes, studio, and boating, underwater, and architectural photography throughout the United States and Europe. His photographs are in private collections and have been used in various advertisements and commercial ventures. Larry resides in Kingston NH as he continues on his photographic journey!

Back cover photograph and watercolor "Bone in her Teeth, schooner *Green Dragon* reaching in a November Nor'wester," by Phyllis Bezanson, painted as a birthday gift for the skipper of *Green Dragon*, fifteen years after their marriage, which took place on the boat, under sail, in calmer seas.

Chesapeake Bay born singer and songwriter Bruce Myers graciously contributed his lyrics to this book. To learn more about Bruce and his music visit his website at http://www.brucemyersmusic.com.

Al Roper, one of the founders of the Great Chesapeake Bay Schooner Race, kindly permitted the use of his lyrics as well.

The fleuron used throughout the book is the sign of the historic Green Dragon Tavern in Boston, the inspiration for the naming of *Green Dragon*. The image as well as a detailed paper model of this hotbed of the American Revolution can be downloaded at www.delta7studios.com/greendragon.htm .

Dedication

To Elizabeth Dunbar, "Liz," a boat owner and sailor and a dedicated teacher who never failed to come to my rescue.

Tale of the *Green Dragon*

> I met an old man on an old pier
> The lines on his face could not hide the years
> He was full of stories of the wind and the sea
> I'd have listened just as long
> As he'd of talked to me.
>
> "Old Boats," Bruce Meyers, *Stinkpot & Rags*

Let me tell you a whale of a tale of two old codgers who liked to sail; one was named Jay, the other one Al. Between them, they had 150 years of life and over 100 years of sailing. Each had only one working eye, and all conversations were in triplicate because both were hard of hearing. I guess that's why they say gentlemen never sail closer to the wind than their age. Her owner skipper Allan Bezanson is a true New England vagabond sailor. Raised in Massachusetts, his playground was the New England coast: fog, high tides, strong currents, and granite were his playmates. I, Jay Irwin, on the other hand, grew up on the Chesapeake Bay with no real tides, current, or fog, just a haze or misty appearance of fog and we can wait it out since it is short-lived and very localized. Thank God for a generally soft bottom.

Being members of the schooner fraternity, Al and I were bound to cross tacks. We met through the Greater Chesapeake Bay Schooner Race. I was the volunteer dock master in Fells Point in Baltimore, the north end and starting point for the race. This race draws schooners from all over the world. We have had one or two from Europe and the *Tole Mour*, a 156-foot three-master from Hawaii. Vessels of all years and types of construction from the hundred-year-old all-wood *Victory Chimes* to steel hulls, fiberglass, and the latest Ferro-cement. With such a diversified fleet participating, I would get phone calls from all over the country asking about lodging, transportation to and from Fells Point, ability to restock the vessel or have minor work performed before the race including docking space and if water, electric, and pump out were available. Some of the vessels were underway off the coast or it might be the home office. Then I got a phone call from Al from his home in Massachusetts saying that his boat was in Oxford, Maryland. It had been trucked down to Oxford so he could cruise the Bay and could he still sign up for the race. This was a real out-of-the-box way to get a schooner down to the Bay for the race. No trouble, just get to Fells Point in time for the pre-race activities. Then we talked about how the weather held him up getting the boat down the coast so he had her trucked. I told him if that were to happen again to call me, for I worked at Markley's boatyard on the western side of the Bay just north of the city, and we could arrange off loading and restepping the sticks and have the *Green Dragon* off to the races. Sure enough the next year Al called, he was in the same predicament and could I gave him the name of a trucker and set everything up at the yard. No biggie. The *Dragon* arrived on a Friday morning. Before lunch she was off-loaded, her bottom painted, spars stepped, running rigging set up, and sailing for Broadway Pier in Fells Point. That started a long-time friendship.

    Now for the true heroine of the tale. She is a true American blue-blooded gaff-rigged schooner conceived and laid down on paper by naval architect Scotty Gannett and built by Chester Spear, both out of Scituate, Massachusetts. Builder Chester Spear turned her lines and scantlings into a solid sound vessel. Her hull is caravel planked mahogany, having a sparred length of 43.6', beam 9.6', and draft 5.6'. Her keel was laid in 1939, but because of World War II her completion and launching didn't come until 1951, sailing under the names of *Lady Millie* and *Brenda Lee*. In 1961, Al saw her spirit and determination and realized she deserved a more appropriate name. She is a true *Green Dragon*, named after the Green Dragon Tavern of Boston that was the headquarters of the Revolution. True to her calling, she stands up to the elements while cradling her crew as a faithful mother would. But we are to ask her to take on one more role, that of a rehabilitation center. Uh, I must confess, uh, I had a full knee replacement uh, about three months earlier, uh, about April 28. Oh, I can walk, climb stairs, step up curbs, drive, and also climb up on a barstool. At the end of two weeks I was going down the pier and out on the finger pier, holding on to the bimini top of my friend's motorboat and stepping to the gunwale, then down in the cockpit, and sitting in a chair. That's right, a motorboat, a chair, like on the sundeck of a house with a basement full of water. Then again, I was boarding my son's yawl climbing over the lifelines, going forward to handle lines. But up here in New England you moor out, traversing in the tender. But here again the *Dragon* came to the rescue. She has the largest porcelain head you will ever find on a boat. It is as large as any one at home, with a teak seat. It's mounted high above the sole; you actually get up on it. You know how on a bar stool your feet just touch the floor, it's easier to keep your feet on the lower rung. Well, this is the same. It even has a footrest. Just the thing for my knee. A handicapped head.

Truly traditional, strip-planked decks, varnished cap rails, green hull, clipper bow, and sawn-off counter. But below, across from the Lunenburg Foundry wood burning stove, she is as modern as any yacht. Sporting an Autohelm 4000, Furno 1623 radar, Furno GP36 DGPS, Garmin 276 chart plotter, and a Raymarine 435I chart plotter out on the binnacle for the helmsman. Keeping with time proven systems, a new Yamnar power plant serviced by a Racor diesel filter/separator was installed below the cockpit in a well laid out spacious compartment serviceable through a "look see" watertight deck inspection hatch. Now, if that is not enough, Al has his laptop PC with an antenna above the deck to reach out to the world. Oh, then also don't forget the cell phone and the Spot Tracker that gives the world our position every ten minutes via the Internet. This allowed Al's friends and my daughters and son to be able to track us as soon as we departed and through the whole day's progress. We can sail but not hide. For the finishing touch, Andy and Amy, Al's son and his girlfriend, had just finished restoring to like new *Snapdragon*, a 10.6' Cape Dory sporting varnished brightwork with green hull.

WAYPOINT 1
L 43° 50' 55" N λ 69° 37' 40" W

And sailing is the answer
To all our lost dreams
It's the answer to the question
Of just what life means
It clears up
What used to be a mystery
All the answers to life
Are in the wind and the sea
  "Generous Return," Bruce Myers,
  Stinkpot & Rags

 The four of us, *Green Dragon*, *Snapdragon*, Al, and I were off on a peregrinate trip. It never entered our minds that we had to be somewhere at a given time, our only timetable was that of tide and current and that was only when it suited our pleasure and convenience. If bit by the sailing bug you get as much pleasure in maintaining the boat, planning the trip, and meeting the people as you do sailing. Clearing Spruce Head, Maine, heading for Boothbay harbor, now under double-reefed main to steady the roll and the mighty power of the Yanmar we were under way; this combination worked very well.
 This area was all new to me. The previous spring Al had asked me if I wanted to sail with him from Willoughby Bay in Norfolk to Mystic Seaport for the 19th Annual Wooden Boat Show event in June. This turned out to be one of those storybook cruises that you always plan for but never seem to get – perfect skies, fair steady winds, and never, I mean never, did the wind go forward of the beam. Most boaters would not believe this tale, for we had logged just under a

thousand miles by the time we dropped the hook in Mystic Seaport. Just a quick rundown of this cruise, we left Willoughby Bay with the destination of Solomon's Island in Chesapeake Bay. Most of the trip north was wing and wing with breaking following seas, then off to a broad reach across the bay jibing over to a close reach straight into Solomon's at the end of the day's air. The following week Al's son and Amy cruised the boat up to Washington, DC. At the end of that week, Al and I picked up the boat at the D.C. Yacht Club and cruised down the Potomac on following air over to Tangier Sound, then another day of light air and beam reaching back to Norfolk. A week later Al, Paul Gray, owner of the schooner *Quintessence*, and I cleared Willoughby Bay heading out of the Chesapeake through the Bay Bridge-Tunnel, then sailing the rhumb line north of Sandy Hook and still the wind abeam or aft. Because of light air from Sandy Hook in, we motored up the East River into Long Island Sound and up to Mystic Seaport. All of this 'gentleman sailing' was in waters and geographical territories that I was comfortable and familiar with. This New England trip now is in new waters, new surroundings, and geographically much different. First, I had to learn how to pick up the mooring right, no slips here (no pun), and how to read the water for rocks just below the surface. Staying clear of lobster buoys is one thing, but lobster boats don't run in a straight line like our Chesapeake Bay crabbers do. They seem to go here, then there, then back again, not necessarily with the current or against it. I just never figured out their reasoning. As we moved through New England, it was so different from the Bay. Each port had its own way of mooring boats. Some had moorings fore and aft to prevent swinging, all in a neat row; others had pilings about sixty feet apart parallel to the shore, each boat moored between them.

    Al would show me the chart and explain where we were going, show me good anchorages, shortcuts between rivers, and tell me of other times he had sailed here. At each harbor

Al knew just where to buy the best bread and get the best pizzas and always knew someone or they knew the boat.
Arriving at Boothbay is like sailing into a postcard. In the foreground is the harbor with commercial fishing vessels, classic yachts, and Tupperware boats of our time. Then in the background up on the railways is *Friendship*, a full size replica of a Salem East Indiaman, spars silhouetted against the backdrop of classic New England homes and shops. Al had acquired the skill and judgment of rounding up to a mooring with perfect confidence, approaching the mooring, staying clear of working tour boats, I was all eyes. A Bristol fashion Friendship sloop working her way through the anchorage under a full head of sail and the schooner *Lazy Jack* reducing sail as she approached her dock to discharge her passengers all the while in very close quarters held my attention.

Thankfully, the mooring belonging to Tugboat Inn Marina which we had previously made arrangements allowing us to moor up to put us in a very favorable spot to go ashore. Here amongst this fine display of seamanship and placid surroundings, I the gimp had to disembark so we could go to dinner. Each time we had to board the tender, Al would move it under the stern counter so I could board. Not being sure of knee and leg, I first had to get around the boom gallows and get my legs outboard on the stern rail, one leg down further than the other as I turned feeling for the tender's seat. Then, holding fast, I'd move my other leg down to find the bottom of the tender, all the time hoping that I did not tip over *Snapdragon* sending Al and me into the drink. Once seated amidships the only thing then was to keep my knee away from Al's outstretched arms as he rowed. At the Tugboat Inn Marina's dinghy dock, Al jumped out with painter in hand and held *Snapdragon* tight against the dock. Now like a cat but not as agile, I was on all fours crawling forward, then out onto the dock still on all fours - certainly not seamanlike but at last I could stand upright, on an even keel able to blend in with the crowd. Al had been here on his way north out of Gloucester and he had a favorite restaurant, Boathouse Bistro (Tapas, pizza, etc.), which served his favorite pizza and had his favorite place to sit. The waiters would always accommodate him. First a martini, relax, take in the view, socialize, and then eat. On the stroll back to the boat we would stop at the fudge stand and get one piece to finish off the night. Back at the tender, everything in reverse but oh so gently.

Next morning a beautiful sunny June day, light steady air, harbor full of activity. After a leisurely breakfast, with Al on the main, me at the fore, we removed gaskets, cleared sheets, hauled away on halyards, and adjusted throat and peak. Motor warmed up, Al nodded, I went forward to throw off the mooring and Al nodded again, turning the wheel so we would fall off on starboard tack; this would allow us to pass astern of the moored boats ahead of us. Everything by the book, routine. "Oh sh__, there goes my hat," a wide-brimmed straw hat setting high on the water presenting good windage for the downwind trek. Al calling, 'Get the boat hook! I'll jibe, run down, and fetch it." Grabbing the boat hook, watching the hat, and seeing Al's course through the anchorage, I moved to the starboard bow. The Friendship sloop and *Lazy Jack* were also setting sail. We jibed and started downwind. Now a fair distance ahead and to port was the *American Eagle*'s dock. Further on were shallow water and a footbridge across the head of the harbor. Now it was time to harden up on port, then head up to motor up to the hat on starboard. Al yelling, "What's wrong with the main?" I, on the bow to fetch the hat, realized it was just out of reach. Al put the boat in reverse making the bow fall off, but not soon enough. The hat sailed on past. Spinning around from a port tack to a starboard tack, we were now heading downwind parallel to the hat but with two moored boats between us. With the help of the motor we were faster than the hat. While coming around on port tack, hat to weather starboard side, I realized the foresheet was fouled on the horse. Freeing it with boat hook in hand and going forward while watching the hat and seeing Al's course through the anchorage, I felt like a one-armed paperhanger in a windy room. Now running downwind with the motor and the sail, we were getting ahead of the hat. Hardening up again and coming head to wind, hat on starboard side to windward, I had time to hook it, Al asking again, "What's wrong with the main?" Oh no! The gooseneck had come apart in the first jibe. The nut had fallen off, and the boom was hanging loose, putting all the weight on the sail. Meanwhile the other boats had stood off watching and waiting. Well, we sure showed them how to execute a Chinese fire drill. I guess they thought we were just two old dudes on a bareboat charter, green horns.

WAYPOINT 2
L 45° 50' 38" N λ 69° 38' 47" W

Well you can say just what you like
About the life I lead
I just don't care
'cause I have all I need
you know that life is just a game
and in the end we all wind up the same
you've got to have fun while you're here
that's what I believe
> "Everybody Go Sailing," Bruce Myers, *Stinkpot and Rags*

Low tide was in the morning so I could really get a feeling of what a ten-foot tide range is. Boy, in some places the boat on the plotter was as wide as the white area on the chart that I had to stay in and then all around were huge rocks that if you were tacking at high water you would surely have to read the water right to stay clear of them. Our plotted course took us through the Sheepscot to Wiscasset by way of the Townsend Gut in the Sheepscot, via the Little Sheepscot and Goose Rocks Passage. We never used waypoints or a route, kind of navigated electronically by the seat of our pants. All of this with a favorable current and wind. This type of passage was all new to me. Being able to sail right up to the rocks and ledges and at the same time in such a pristine environment. Al's sailing companion, the indispensable *A Cruising Guide to the New England Coast*, is not only the Bible for gunkholing but gives great little tidbits of information like how schooners used to go into Back River to load ice from Knickerbocher Pond, then have to be towed out backwards.

On days when it's too thick or lumpy out in the Gulf of Maine for your liking, you will often find agreeable conditions in the Sheepscot. The Maine saying "You can't get there from here" doesn't apply when you are in this river, for it is 'wired' with a network of passages from river to river. You can wander for days without going outside.

Wiscasset is on U.S. Route One, and here is where the two old abandoned schooners *Hesper* and *Luther Little* had lain since the Depression. Since the '60s, each time I went north I always stopped, took pictures, and tried to find out more about them. Then in 1995, they were dismantled. Here I was sailing in a schooner to the very spot. Life is good.

The real reason for coming here was to meet Mr. Mudd Sharrigan, a knife maker that Al had met at one of the boat shows. He is known for his sailor knives as well as being a competitive swimmer in his age group (82.) Just as arranged, he was at the pier head to greet us, then off to his home and shop. Out in the garage he explained in great detail how he forged each blade from piles of steel, car springs, lawnmower blades, old band saw blades, even motorcycle chains. He had two gas-fired forges, one of which was a rotary one which gave a faster and more even heat, bringing the steel to the right temperature for hammering to the right consistency and shape on the anvil. Because of the different metals in the chains, the finished blade had a soft design or pattern in it, similar to a snakeskin or fish scales. Blades from motor cycle chains were wider, like a machete or Bowie knife. In his basement on the wall over the workbench were wooden knives, patterns of the knife he was to make, each one hand-carved to get the right handle to blade ratio, shape, and balance. Then he showed us his diversified types of wood for the handles. He is a true artist.

Then again it goes back further, they say birds of a feather flock together. In the early 50's Mr. Mudd was renowned throughout the hot-rodding community as a pioneering founder of the Watertown, MA No-Mads and the New England Hot Rod Council. The No-Mads, working in backyards around Boston, had the coolest custom cars outside California. Mudd's craftsmanship was already evident with his showpiece, a bronze-colored '32 Ford roadster. Al in turn was a Marlboro, MA Piston Pusher, first trying his hand at stock car racing in a '34 Ford. I, in turn, down in Baltimore had converted my grandfather's '34 Plymouth coupe into a street rod. Running with the local hot rodders we became known as the Night Crawlers because during after hours in the local garage we built our stock car, #88. So often you run into other boaters who had been or are still car heads. I guess we are the type that likes to be free thinkers and tinker with things, creators of our own destiny.

    A great visit with Mr. Mudd, then down the River with the ebb. We made a side trip into the little cove north of Sawyers Island to scout out the swing bridge at Trevett. Then down alongside Isle of Springs, weaving between small islands until we dropped the hook for the night in Ebencook Harbor, a secure anchorage. Next day off again to Boothbay to see what a suspected hurricane was up to.

WAYPOINT 3
L 43° 59' 57" N λ 69° 39' 52" W

> The sails are up the sheets are tied
> Hold and enjoy the ride
> We're steady getting there
> The rigging's tight the mast is strong
> Heeled and sailing along
> We're steady getting there
>
> "Boat Logic," Bruce Myers, *Stinkpot & Rags*

This time instead of picking up a mooring in Boothbay Harbor, we would work more to the west of the harbor to McKown Point. Sailing in company with another sailor amongst moored boats and the channel getting narrower and narrower, finally we saw our intended mooring and the floating pier belonging to Harborfields Housekeeping Cottages. We had been warned to stand clear of the ledge starboard side as it is shallow. When it was safe, we flopped over on starboard tack, eyeballing a lay line to the mooring, allowing us to enter a small mooring area. Lobster boats, cruising and small sailboats shared the area between a substantial ledge and the floating pier.

This turned out to be a very interesting port of call. Mr. Rick Thorpe, whose great–great-grandfather Charles Thorpe had purchased the property in 1832, had invited Al. Living in a house built in 1870 on over a quarter mile of saltwater shoreline and 8 acres of woods and fields, they raised sheep and cattle and used the property as a base for a fishing operation. Now a 1780 farmhouse, a lodge and 7 fully equipped cottages, along with a dock, floats, boats to rent, and moorings, all with their own special water view, are operated as a friendly vacation resort. Located only two miles by land or a mile across the water from the village of Boothbay, it is a very good place for boats cruising in the area that want to rent a mooring for a layover.

After securing the boat we went ashore to look around; this is my type of place. First, there was a 1937 or '39 International pick-up in original condition. I am sure used to run into town with or just maybe to work around the property. All types of boats in all kinds of condition and years were stashed everywhere. One poor old 35-footer was over on her beam ends looking like a dead whale. Instead of being cut in and tried out for her oil from a staging, there was a young man on a ladder cutting her up with a cordless reciprocating saw only to be taken to the dump. She should have been left to sink with dignity or laid up in some old marsh to become a habitat for wildlife and decay back into nature. How many paintings or photographs have you seen of some old derelict? Now you view it in a whole new spectrum of a vessel. Beauty is in the eye of the beholder.

Al, Mark Standley, and another friend, Fred, had helped Mr. Thorpe sail his 44-foot Catalina sloop to Annapolis the previous fall. This was like a reunion: *Green Dragon* working her way south, Mr. Standley's sloop *Jezebel* out for a cruise, and Mr. Thorpe sailing around in any one of his choice of his boats here. Mark Standley and his wife Janet were to pick up their son and cruise in the same area Al and I had passed through.

Listening to Al and Mark talk over areas to sail through and places to anchor during Mark's trip was amazing. Each knew the area like the back of his hand. One would mention a place and the other one would see it in his mind's eye and comment on the pros and cons. What the wind and seas would be like in this or that passage if the hurricane did develop. If the hurricane did stay off shore and only create rain, which port or anchorage would be preferred? One would mention an anchorage and the other would comment what protection and from what quarter it would offer. Each knew his boat and knew how much discomfort he was willing to endure.

A very social atmosphere was everywhere throughout the camp. We were invited to dinner and breakfast at Mr.Thorpe's and two other times dinner at homes of other guests. During one of the conversations at dinner, one of the guests mentioned he had just bought special plywood for his Ford "Woody," which he was keeping in top shape. That started a conversation leading to the fact that he had a 1936 Ford roadster in his barn, his wife commenting 'yes, instead of a horse in the stall.'

The property being a family vacation camp, children were everywhere - on a rope swing, sailing, kayaking, rowing, and fishing off the floating pier. Now they say that you can catch mackerel and striped bass; well, from what I saw caught I am sure glad Al had plenty of peanut butter aboard. Wherever you were people would start up a conversation, where they had been, where they wanted to go. Boats always, the difference between a round chine lobster boat and the hard chine bay deadrise, should a wood bottom be sealed with resin or just painted the old way. Afternoons and evenings were cocktail time in the cockpit of one of the boats and spilling over onto the dock. Out on *Green Dragon* at low tide, the ledge east of us became quite a landmass blocking the view to Boothbay. For me this was very different, and I am sure the locals who have never been in Chesapeake Bay country could not understand my concern. Here and everywhere we had people seeming to sail in close quarters a lot more than at home. They were sailing between us and the ledge, in and out of the harbor, on and off the pier. At home I am one of the few who likes to sail in and out of my slip if the wind is right, and I prefer to sail up and down the river instead of motoring. Another thing I noticed was that many of people here were full families - parents, children, and grandchildren. This made conversations easy as

Al and I both sail with our children and grandchildren. In fact, Al's grandchild Nathan had crewed for Al on the trip north.

During all of this socializing Al and Mark were constantly watching the weather on their computers, tracking the approach of Hurricane Bill. Both thought the biggest threat was heavy rain. A lot of this high tech instrument sailing and weather reading is kind of out of my league. I'm kind of a seat of the pants sailor. None of my boats had a depth finder or radio until the kids gave me a radio in case my wife needed medical help. I always had full-scale charts, *Chart No. 1*, *Eldridge Tide and Pilot Book* or tide and current tables of the bay on board. A hand- bearing compass, stopwatch, and navigation tools got all of us everywhere we wanted, day or night.

Using the internet for weather and sea conditions puts you right in the driver's seat for a safe and pleasant voyage, a chance to set the right sails and have the smaller ones secured on deck ready for the change. Old routines and ingrained habits are hard to bury. My mentors were old salts who came up through the hawse pipe on tired old wood vessels that didn't take kindly to being driven hard through foul weather. They had taught me to look up at the masthead flies checking wind direction and strength as you walked down the pier to the boat. Check the pilings for tide range, and how moored boats lay with the current, or the tail of the current around pilings for direction. Before Weather Cubes, we kept the radio on an AM station so it could pick up the static from a "thunderhead." If we saw Cumulus clouds early in the day we knew to keep a sharp eye to the northwest, for the Cumulus were forerunners for Cumulo-nimbus and when they formed an anvil on their tops, look out, you were forced to reduce sail and get ready for a real storm. It's still fun watching the sky and trying to figure out or make a calculated guess of the advancing weather. Now you have the ability to see the weather maps and what's happening west of you, and it makes you feel good that you had kind of predicted the future weather. Up until now most of the trip has been under sunny clear skies with cool temperatures under "woolpack clouds," or "fair weather" Cumulus. Right now we had a "mackerel sky" and a good chance this could change into the predicted rain.

Al and the rest of the guys here were old school so both systems were constantly in use. That's why we could move about in fog or clear weather, in and out of channels cut close to ledges, or lay a course across open water with assurance that we were where we thought we were and still be safe. Many times while at the wheel I was sure glad that I could look down at the plotter and see just where we were instead of having to plot our position. A quick look at the chart, then the plotter, is sure easy. Also, the projected rhumb line on the plotter is a big help for how far you can carry the course you are on. Being able to zoom in and out on the plotter, I could see if the course we were on would clear all obstacles ahead or how soon we would have to alter course. I guess this old dog has learned new tricks.

Al had been watching the weather daily on the internet and calling it right all along, which is the reason for such a pleasant trip up to this point. I had watched Al use the computer forecasting sailing conditions for the next or following days on other trips, such as when we delivered the boat north from Norfolk with the wind abaft and pleasant sea conditions. If the approaching hurricane did develop as expected, producing only heavy rain, Mr. Thorpe's mooring that we were on was more than heavy enough to hold the *Dragon* during such a hurricane. Being surrounded on three sides to the west of the mooring by high ground will give adequate protection. To the east the ledge would break up any sea developed because of the mile-long fetch of open water which could build quite a sea.

No big deal, we could stay on Mr. Thorpe's mooring. If the hurricane brought the expected amount of rain, Al felt that *Green Dragon*'s decks shipped too much water for us to live aboard. He said I would be soaked sleeping in the forepeak under the deck. I tried to explain that I had slept many times in full foul weather gear or had used a sail for a blanket. But a wise decision was made.

WAYPOINT 4
L 43° 50' 39" N λ 69° 38' 46" W

When I think of all the friends I used to have
All the times that we once had
We all went our separate ways
To pay the dues we all must pay
There must be a reason
But what it is I am not sure
And I'm living life underway
Ship to shore
      "Boat Logic," Bruce Myers, *Stinkpot & Rags*

  Now that we had decided to leave the boat to fend for herself, I would call my daughter Denise who lives in Northport, Maine, not too far north of Boothbay. This will give us some time together to jaw about my latest sailing adventures. Denise is my first child and has been sailing longer than life. Her mother was nine mouths pregnant when she and I were learning to sail on a twenty-foot sloop. My wife and her best friend, who was also in her ninth month, would hike out on the high side; that way we got the advantage of four in place of two. Denise has always been my sidekick, and the pair of us have sailed many miles through all kinds of weather. Whether racing, cruising, or just out on the river for a spin, we both wanted the proper sail hanked on for the air we had and constantly trimmed to get the maximum out of the boat. Many a day we would roam through boatyards checking out other people's boats or finding friends who might be working or just messing around like us. The area around Northport, Camden, Rockland, and Belfast are communities along U.S. Route One and connected by Penobscot Bay, not a bad area to roam around during our lay-up. So between rain showers my sidekick and I went off to find some of the working schooners, hoping to track down some of the crewmembers we knew. In '07 I had sailed from Spruce Head to Camden with Al to do the Eggemoggin Reach Regatta.

This was my first introduction to New England sailing. From Camden we sailed north to Castine, the home of the Maine Maritime Academy and the schooner *Bowdoin*, a very interesting boat. I had gotten a book of her history in a bookstore in Rockport in the season of 2000 when here on the tugantine *Norfolk Rebel* with Captain Lane Briggs. I had been following her for many years in magazines but had never had the chance to board her or even see her. Then in a bookstore in Rockport, Maine, I found *The Arctic Schooner Bowdoin*, a biography by Virginia Thorndike. I had sailed into Rockport at the end of the Tall Ship Regatta during the season of 2000 on the tugantine *Norfolk Rebel* with Captain Lane Briggs and by chance wandered into a coffee shop and bookstore. Now I know the rest of the story. *Bowdoin* had been built to a design and construction for an unusual mission, that of sailing in northern waters not yet charted or sailed in by other explorers. Her first trip higher than the Arctic Circle was in August, 1921. Now under the ownership of the Maine Maritime Academy she was preparing, in Thorndike's words, "to return to her own milieu, the North." What a way to find her, seeing her from the deck of an old gaffer and finding her in tip top shape readying for another trip north.

Back to arriving in Castine. As we sailed up to the yacht club, we realized we were going to sail into a race and the approaching yachts were working to weather. Our course would cross ahead of them, putting us to weather of them. Dipping to starboard hard indicated we would stand clear and cross astern of the fleet. As the first boat passed us, an elderly gentleman at the tiller looked over at us and nodded a high sign indicating his approval of our intention and action. With that Al said, "Do you know who you just gave right of way to?"

"Hell no, I'm impressed with the boats. What are they, New York thirty-twos?"

"I don't know, but that is Olin Stevens and this whole regatta is celebrating him as a designer, racer, and he has just turned ninety. How many racing champions has he designed, not counting the cruising yachts?"

Later I was sure glad that I could recognize him and not make a fool of myself. Leaving Castine we raced back to Camden, air too light for a gaffer so iron jenny with fore and main. The next race hosted by *WoodenBoat* magazine was from Camden to Broken, Maine. We had met up with the schooner *Heron* out of New Jersey, owned and completely rebuilt by Bobby Pulsch. In fact, his crew had met up with us the day we arrived in Camden.

Well, at the start of the race, it was dead still. *Heron* and the *Dragon* had picked the same end of the starting line. As we drifted close to *Heron* Al yielded over to Bobby, stating that it was a long haul to Broken and sure looked like an iron jenny day. So off we went. You know, motor sailing is not that bad if you want to sightsee and enjoy watching the other boats. We were in a fleet of old wooden classic boats that are always a pleasure to watch. Boy, some of those jibe-headed old girls could sure point and move nicely on such light air. As we worked our way through cuts and between islands we were always in company of other schooners, some out on a charter, others like the schooner *Winfield Lash,* another friend of Al's heading like us for Broken. Now here is another great tale of how Dave Clarke built her and his sailing adventures. Maybe on another watch. Arriving at and anchoring off *WoodenBoats* frontage in Broken put us in the middle of the action for the Eggemoggin Reach Regatta. There will be ninety boats at the start all types, sizes, all in

Bristol fashion. Well now, this is the area Denise, Fred, and I will be roaming around in by car. The thing about pulling into marinas or boat yards by car is that you are a tourist. The only way to save face is if by chance you meet some past crewmember or an acquaintance of one of your sailing friends.

I had my daughter pick me up and I went back to Northport, ME with her. Al went home to be with his wife and clean up some unfinished business. Retuning a little too soon, Al found it was wet and cold aboard and no dry firewood for the stove. When I arrived back at the boat, the sky was clear and the forecast gave each of us the feeling to move on.

Departing from Mr. Thorpe's mooring we headed for Boothbay Harbor, this time for the town dock as we were only to pick fresh foods and last minute ship stores. Being Sunday and in the early morning, there was no trouble finding a space on the floating pier. By the time we were ready to leave the harbor and town it had become very active. Now the area by the floating pier was a lot more congested and we had a large motor vessel abeam of us that was taking on passengers. With a little forethought and rearranging of lines, we were able to warp the *Dragon* around so her head was towards open water. This time we dipped our hats, bid our farewells, and departed properly.

Off again to York, Maine, and Annisquam (Gloucester) by Isles of Shoals. The run to York Harbor was somewhat uneventful but always in the company of lobster boats. At one point we were steaming along and as we approached a lobsterman working ahead of us he would cross our rhumb line from port to starboard, then back again, each time making a breaking wake in one area which was also in the vicinity of a mark. Now there was very little air and no seas. I looked at the plotter to find the mark and depth. The way we had been going around islands and working between ledges, I was never sure if we were going up river or down. Not knowing which side to take the mark till I did identify it I looked at the plotter to find out. Checking the plotter I asked Al if he knew what was up ahead.

"No, what's up?"

"Something is making the water break just ahead of us where that lobster boat's wake is." Just at that time I found the mark and started to port, which was the right decision. We were on the back side, the intended channel and the rock pile was between us and the mark running off to our starboard.

Once around the mark we felt much better and thanked Neptune for the calm seas, which made the breaking wake stand out. You sure have to pay attention and constantly read the water. The rest of the day the air was light and we were on a falling tide. Closer to York we were working our way up the channel watching for the shoals off Stage Neck and Bragdon Island. About here is a "submerged pile," as they say up here, but not breaking or visible at the shoalest part. With this, we were beckoned by a passing lobster boat to move over and give the shoal more berth.

The *Cruising Guide* said the current runs very hard on flood and ebb, recommending picking up a mooring from the harbormaster so the mooring would be the right weight for the boat. Entering the harbor we motored through the anchorage but decided to call the harbormaster as advised. Within minutes, he called back and said he would be over to lead us to a mooring. After making sure we were secured, he lay along side and chatted for quite awhile. Being real impressed with the *Green Dragon,* he wanted to know everything about her. In conversation, he told us that he had been in Baltimore at Curtis Bay during his hitch in the Coast Guard and knew of The Block in Baltimore, a real sailor's Fiddlers Green – an earthly sort of "sensual Elysium." After assuring him that we did not care to go ashore and needed nothing more that evening, he still offered his service as long as he was on duty. Later that evening as we sat in the cockpit with an evening drink you could surely see the strength of the current. The mooring buoys and the mark at the end of the bar were laid over on their sides half submerged. During the full run of the current, the locals moved about in every size or type of boat, always making the right correction allowing for set and drift. Upstream of us there seemed to be a fair amount of commercial fishing boats. Some were the old harpooner types with the unbelievably long bowsprit or pulpit. The captain's steering station is high on a tuna tower so he has a clear view of the sea ahead of him so he can see the swordfish on the surface. Sliding down a cable fastened over his head going down to the pulpit is the fastest way to the end of the pulpit from which he harpoons the fish. The harpoon is very long with a small barrel or float attached which the fish will tow along if harpooned, causing him to tire out fast and also to mark him. I had seen these boats working out of Indian River, New Jersey. This whole area was very active, people walking along a promenade hand in hand, walking dogs, biking, or just power exercising. As I sat in the cockpit taking in the activities and strength of the current, my mind went back to the anchorage in St. Leonard Creek off the Patuxent River down on the Chesapeake the previous spring. Here the water seemed not to show any movement between high and low water. The park just off our starboard was very quiet with only a few people milling around. Here was the *Dragon* all alone, lying at anchor at the headwaters where the wetlands and marsh started and the entire length of the river downstream bordered only by private homes or farms. The only commercial activity was an old gravel or sand pit off-loading onto barges. Time seemed to stand still. So did the current the following morning, which made retrieving the anchor a snap.

WAYPOINT 5
L 44° 20' 07" N λ 68° 58' 04" W

Some old boats are classrooms now
And some old boats museums
Some old boats rest on the bottom
Breeding grounds for crabs and clams
  "Old Boats," Bruce Myers, *Stinkpot & Rags*

    As we approached Isles of Shoals, Gosport we sailed in under Appledore Island, through or around the small harbor surrounded by Smutty Nose, Cedar, and Star Island. What an interesting place. Other captains had been there, but explorer Captain John Smith in 1614 named them after himself "Smythe Islands." Its abundance of fish brought the first settlers. Land speculators Ferdinando Gorges and John Mason were granted royal title. Potential profits from fishing were so great the investors divided the property, half of the Isles of Shoals ending up in New Hampshire, the other half in Maine. In 1732 isolated from mainland laws, manners, and religion, the population became hard drinkers. Now the main island, Star, is owned by the Universalist Unitarian Church, which has a large hotel on the site. But outsiders cannot stay overnight; they must be off the island by nightfall, a hundred and eighty degrees turnaround from the old days.
    Cruising along at times in fog but mostly sunny weather, and Al giving the history of each area, the whole time in the company of lobster boats and other cruisers. Now about this fog. Al and I weren't the only ones handicapped. *Green Dragon* had a flaw herself. The compass had a large air bubble naturally right on top just under the binnacle light. No big deal in daylight, just a reference point if needed, but in fog, real fog, you really need to see the exact course. At first I tried using the plotter, no way. It has a delay because of the

signals and the swaying of the antenna changes the direction too fast. Just not used to it. Boy, at first we were heading every which way, our wake would sure break the snake's back. Nothing to do except sit directly astern of the binnacle, pay attention, let the other one be lookout. We had a great sail down Ipswich Bay to the Annisquam River.

Entering the river at low tide with an adverse current was an advantage. First, if we grounded we would not have too long to pound or sit on bottom. Second, with the current running at low water it's easier to read the water. You'll see the eddies or different wave patterns from the disturbance from the rocks below. Once in the river, around one or two bends watching and giving way to other vessels, all of a sudden we were passing Annisquam Yacht Club, where we were to pick up Mr. Standley's mooring as he and his wife were off cruising on *Jezebel*. Passing by and sight-seeing, we took a pass through the anchorage checking out all the different types of boats, looking over the town, and just enjoying the end of the day's sail. Readying the boat to pick up the mooring just in front of the club, we were in a field of small boats, some tacking up and down the river, kayaks, inflatables, and small motorboats crisscrossing back and forth from a beach just abeam of our intended mooring, each one checking us out, waving, and giving us the high sign. The *Dragon* sure is a head turner. Pay attention, we are picking up a club mooring, look sharp! Annisquam Yacht Club is a large building on pilings and rock cribs over the water. Just to the left of it, or downriver side, was a large mud flat. At low tide, the rowboats and tenders anchored here were settled on the mud waiting for the flood.

  The town or community behind the yacht club was a true New England town. The layout and design of the homes made a crazy patchwork design. Some houses were frame-built square box types, I believe called saltboxes, built in the 1700s. Others were stone made at a much later date. That evening we took the tender to the yacht club's floating dock and walked around town.

It is so neat to roam around another man's town. Some of the homes had the year they were built over the doorway. One home had a transom nameboard of some vessel over the threshold; others had trailboards on their walls. Along Leonard Street to the corner of Cambridge Avenue was a sculptured hedge that from its height and width you could tell was very old, yet sculpted into the interesting design. Another piece of property had a large old tree that looked like a live oak, but we were informed by Al's daughter that live oaks do not grow this far north. Next day we took the tender to Wingaersheek Beach across from our mooring and painted her identification in her hull. (T/T *Green Dragon*) just in case she wandered off on her own. The following day we tacked upriver to the Route 128 bridge just before Gloucester, came about, and sailed back down with current and wind, oh to run free wing and wing at times, oh to be free! Clearing Annisquam River back into Ipswich Bay, light air, foul current, but reaching. As each cove passed to leeward, Al would name them: Hodgkin's Cove, Plum Cove, then Lane's Cove.

Now there's always one time or place that stands out and you are so glad to be there and part of it. Al told me of a stone quarry – Lane's Cove – that looked just like the ones in Ireland (I guess because that's where the stonecutters and masons came from.) As we approached with the current on the bow, I saw the little opening no wider than our total length, Al saying, "Be careful of the current as you go in!" In, under sail; oh boy. As we entered we were set at an angle making the stern almost touch the granite, Al hauled the main boom in to clear. Now the harbor was full of moorings with boats, and the moorings were chained to the granite quay making it impossible to round them. Main pushed hard to weather, engine in reverse, then forward, then reverse, then forward, main sheeted in, bow coming around, and out we sailed. Clearing the narrow entrance, Al said, "All of that and no-one saw us. Oh well." Cleared, we headed for Rockport sailing past Folly Cove, then sailing between two large rocks on Halibut Point, admiring the home here with stone statues and beautiful rock work. Working south, we tacked close to the entrance to Pigeon Cove so I could see the Inner Harbor, another place Al was used to sailing into. Then out into the open water tacking with another sailor down to Rockport. Now here again we entered a small entrance only to find the harbor full, but here they moor the boats fore and aft with a fairway down to the head of the harbor. Right at the head is the Sandy Beach Yacht Club. With the ten-foot tide, which was at low water, the club sat high on a set of pilings, yes, ten feet above us. They had us lay beam to, fender boards to keep us off, long bow and stern lines, long spring lines springs fore and aft. When they saw the *Dragon*, no way were they going to put us on a mooring.

It seemed everyone knew Al and the *Dragon*. As we were working the boat alongside, throwing lines up to the handlers as they in turn sent down the long fender boards, the whole time the current running, there was a woman our age in a kayak standing just off our stern. As soon as all docking was done, she came up alongside, handing me a dirty, peaked baseball cap saying I might like to have it. Taking it, I thanked her, not really looking at it, and put it down and finished squaring away all lines. Later Al said, "Where did this hat come from?" Wow. It's a hat from the *Green Dragon* that participated in the Around the World race that had been in Boston on one of its stops. That's right; she said she had fished it out of Boston Harbor. Damn. This is probably one of the crew's; it sure looked like it had been around the world! Off I went to find her, but like the morning mist she had cleared the harbor.

First a shower, then hooking up with a co-worker of Al's, we walked over to Rockport's Bearskin Neck to get a highly recommended hot dog at the Top Dog of Rockport.

Back on the deck of the Yacht Club, we had a perfect view of the old red fishing shack Motif No. 1. It is instantly recognized because of innumerable paintings and prints. Because of the recognition, it is considered one of the most famous buildings in the world. That evening the entertainment from the yacht club deck was Small Boat Race Night so there were boats sailing in and out of the harbor all evening. It was some show as they sailed off the moorings, through the anchorage, then back again after the race. About that time a friend of Al's said "Hey, didn't you sail into Lane's Cove?" He had been in the clubhouse and they had a security web cam for the harbor. Sure enough, he had seen us come in and work our way out. Damn, Al! No one has done that since the last time you did it and how many years has that been? So someone had seen us after all, another tale to be told.

WAYPOINT 6
L 42° 39' 05" N λ 70° 40' 46" W

It's fine to have a blow-out in a fancy restaurant,
With terrapin and canvas-back and all the wine you want;
To enjoy the flowers and music, watch the pretty women pass,
Smoke a choice cigar, and sip the wealthy water in your glass.
It's bully in a high-toned joint to eat and drink your fill,
But it's quite another matter when you
      Pay the bill
    Robert W. Service, *Best Of the Yukon*

  Off to Gloucester for the 25th Gloucester Schooner Festival. Now Gloucester to me is a great place, the true schooner capital of the world. It's here that started the schooner movement as we know it today. The days of fishing, freighting, design, construction, racing, and the development of the American schooner men. I'll admit many schooner crews came from Nova Scotia and Labrador, but it's here they had the chance to work and sail on such a diversified fleet. My first trip here was aboard the tugantine *Norfolk Rebel* under Captain Lane Briggs. It was at the end of the Tall Ships Challenge Event in 2000. We came to participate in the Gloucester Schooner Festival, seems like a repeat. Now here's another tale. The book and movie *The Perfect Storm* had been out. I had seen the movie but not read the book. While Lane and I were shopping for groceries, I bought the book *Perfect Storm*. Returning to the *Rebel*, in the tender we motored past *Adventure*, which was on the railway being rebuilt. With that, someone called down, "Captain

Lane." It was the now captain, or custodian, of *Adventure*. In conversation with Captain Lane, he mentioned he had been showing guests how cod were cleaned, salted, and stored while out on the Banks in the day of fishing. "Would you like a couple of heads for dinner, Cap?" Lane looked at me, saying, "Would you like some?" "If you know how to fix them, sure." Throwing the heads into the grocery bag, we were off. Back on *Rebel* stowing away the ship's stores, out came the salted fish heads and my now salted new book. D___! Just got it, not a page read. But wait, what better way than to read such a book right from Gloucester salted from a cod head off the *Adventure*. It is one of my favorite treasures.

When entering Gloucester harbor, off to starboard you will see iconic old frame buildings still sporting white letters advertising Gloucester Seajacket Marine Paints Manufactory, 1863. Here is where the first anti-fouling paint was invented. It's also the tip of Rocky Neck, one of America's oldest art colonies. There are so many firsts here, or at least things that were on the cutting edge at that time. Gloucester is such a fascinating place for maritime heritage. The Burnham Brothers Railway, built in 1849, is believed to be the first marine railway. Possibly copied after the railroad that ran from Boston to Gloucester, it is the oldest continuously working marine railway in the country. Gloucester was the largest fishing port in the western hemisphere after the Civil War. It's the home of the *Adventure*, the famous Essex-built dory fishing schooner that outlasted men capable of dory fishing. Famous dory fisherman Howard Blackburn's Halibut Point bar and restaurant is here. The Crow's Nest, the bar featured in *The Perfect Storm*, is here. Gorton's, one of the oldest fish processing plants in the country, owned the fishing schooner *Esperanto*, which took two straight wins from the Canadian fishing schooner *Delawanna* in the First International Fishermen's Race at Halifax, Nova Scotia. Gloucester is just a great liberty port with some really good museums on maritime heritage. A must is the statue *Man at the Wheel* and now the new statue of *Widow and Child* staring out at the sea.

With *Green Dragon* being moored out or rafted, I would go ashore with Al, then we would part, he to take care of business or see friends, I off to the Laundromat, then to my old haunts Old Timers, Rum Line, Halibut Point, and the Crow's Nest. Each time I'm in town I go down to the Seven Seas Wharf to see Tom Ellis and his wife Kay and get the latest news about their schooner *Thomas E. Lannon*, which is in the charter business, always sailing full and by through the harbor. This year George Walls, owner-skipper of the schooner *Amica*, teamed up with me, so I had two tenders to get about in. For the rest of the story about books, in '01 I was on one of my trips around town and I had stopped at the Dory Shop, then down to the railway to chat with the crew rebuilding *Adventure*. One of the crew took me aft and had me stand at the wheel. Wow! You can feel the indentation in the deck where so many crewmen had stood when on the helm. This is one section of deck they hope will never be replaced. After leaving the railway, I just started walking. Next thing, I was entering the Dog Town Bookstore at 2 Duncan Street. Just walking around, not really thinking of buying a book, I picked up *Adventure, Queen of the Windjammers*, by Joseph Garland with Captain Jim Sharps. What a book! What a story! What a boat!

Picking up our mooring just off the Coast Guard station put us right in the middle of the Schooner Festival. Now it was our turn to sit back, all eyes and attention to size up the super-schooners. I like to study the rigging and layout, you can really learn from the professionals. Some heavy hitters were there: *Alabama, American Eagle, Bluenose II, Liberty Clipper, Peacemaker, Pride of Baltimore II, Roseway, Spirit of Bermuda, Unicorn,* and *Virginia*, not counting the seven or eight smaller schooners. Now last year Al gave a beer party for the Canadian crew on *Bluenose II* with the invitation B.Y.O.B (Bring Your Own Boat). It was so well received that he was about to do the same this year, can you imagine a crew that size on the *Green Dragon*? Being here changed our lifestyle and timetable. *Green Dragon* was to be put in harness, off to work. She had to be at the starting line at the precise time, then off and running like Seabiscuit or Man o' War to beat the clock at the finish line. The wind and seas were just right for us. Wind right at the point where you were thinking should I reef or not, we didn't. Waves, some whitecaps, with easy rollers. The course two-mile legs, two times around, reach up and reach down, true schooner point of sail.

Like at all race starts, everybody is tacking back and forth, jumping under your stern, or sliding just under your bow. All the time you are fascinated at the handling and sailing qualities of the other boats. Jeff Robinson's *Phra Luang* had a set of sails that looked like they were painted on. Not a wrinkle, not a flaw. Al's son Andy had taken the wheel and was captain of the day. He had a good background in small boat racing and grew up on the *Dragon*, so he had no trouble keeping her trimmed and balanced to get the most out of the air and sea conditions, having Al trimming, fine-tuning, and getting the best out of her. Amy and I were sheet handlers. There's something about working the boat in close quarters and using other boats as the pace setters. Each tack or trim we worked in unison. The *Dragon* responded, showing her pleasure or displeasure. All in all, we took a second to *Phra Luang*. But she had sailed with an elapsed time of 2:36:45 whereas *American Eagle* under John Foss was winner of Big Boats with an elapsed time of 2:27:55, only an eight-minute ten-second spread; not bad if you have to take second. Then again, second place is the first one to lose- but at least a first.

Now most landlubbers will tell you sailing is 90% boredom with 10% sheer terror and chaos. Well, we had our share. We had left the mooring to raft up with George Wells'

Amica, which had rafted to *Perception*, I think, which in turn had made fast to a large barge. Now the barge's intended use was for schooners to moor to. Some time in the middle of the night there was a loud bang up on deck as if something had dropped from aloft. Jumping up, the four of us sprang on deck. Nothing. Nothing from aloft, nothing had collided with us, no one had fallen. Al jumped into the tender to see if something or someone had gone overboard. "Oh, s..., we're hung up on a piling!" The bowsprit is up on a piling and the boat is at a 30-degree angle. Andy joined his dad in the tender to see just what he meant. Amy and I were told to stand on the stern rail to raise the bow, no such luck. Then we realized we were only at half tide, which meant we would be dropping another five feet, 'way too much strain on the bowsprit and rig. Perched on the stern rail, Amy and I could hear them saying "D__n, the bobstay hung up first, then the bobstay split the piling, letting the boat fall hanging up on the end of the bowsprit." It was dead center on the piling. After several tries of ways to free her, out came a small saw. They cut away at the piling, warning each other to stay clear as they did not know which side would break away first, left or right. With that the sound of splitting wood, the sound of the whisker stay as if strummed as on a guitar, rigging shaking, bow dropping, Amy and I holding on tight to the boom, one big drop, splash, and the *Dragon* was free. Now the question: how did we get into this position? No way were we close to that piling when we turned in last night. Something had moved, surely not the piling. We were still rafted against *Amica*, fenders in place, springs in place. So what moved? The barge that was put there temporarily to accommodate the visiting schooners is the one that had moved during the high tide. Sure enough, when we checked the spuds on the piling, they were up with the wedges in place. If the spuds were driven down into the bottom, the wedges would not be in place so the barge could rise on the flood, and then settle on the ebb. A close look and no real damage. Whisker stay hull fittings had pulled loose and screw holes elongated, but all in all, with a little work we could have her sailing and feel safe until we got to Crocker's, the yard that did all the major work on the *Dragon*.

We all have our own personal personalities and traits, and *Green Dragon* is no different from the crew. This hanging up thing seems to be one of her hang-ups. It seems she wants to be as free as a fire-breathing dragon. Last year while wintering in Norfolk a head wind came up, making the *Green Dragon* lay back on her mooring lines. It seems that the aft springline slipped and she was allowed to come further back into the slip. As the tide fell, her main boom hung up on the dock astern. Snap! Now a new boom was surely in order. It seems she just doesn't like to be kept in stocks.

Gloucester and the Festival was great social entertainment. Friday Mayor's Reception for Invited Guests, Saturday All Hands Party, Sunday Parade of Sail, then the start of the Mayor's Race followed by the reception and awards ceremony. In between all of this we were visiting other schooners, catching up on old news or making new friends. But time moves on, and so should we.

WAYPOINT 7
L 42° 36' 37" N   λ 45° 39' 28" W

Some old boats, they get new motors
Some old motors get new boats
It doesn't matter which way it goes
As long in the end it floats
> "Old Boats," Bruce Myers, *Stinkpot & Rags*

 Monday the weather and current were in our favor so off to Manchester. *Green Dragon* had had her bottom cleaned twice by divers, once in Norfolk and just in Boothbay. Al felt that the anti-fouling was pretty well washed off, and she had a lot more sailing ahead of her. Crocker's, here we come.

 Being creatures of habit, we soon fell into our routines. Let's start with the night before. We would hit the sack relatively early, sometimes a drink first, then read for a while, most times I beat Al to sleep. Me, I'm a soporific addict, a real sack hound. On a boat, I can sleep anytime, any place, and I really enjoy it. But if wakened, I can get right up, perform any task, or give clear answers if needed. I can sleep all day and night. Al, on the other hand, was up very early every morning. It was his time to go out on the internet, find weather conditions, times of tide and current, information about where we were heading, and check email. When I woke up there was a hot cup of coffee. If we had decided the night before to get an early departure, I would rise as I heard Al up. Cup of coffee, warm up the Yammie, raise the double-reefed main, and drop the lines.

 After sun-up, further down the rhumb line, Al would hand out breakfast. If it was to be a slow, lazy day start, we would have breakfast, wash up, and take in the surroundings. En route I was at the wheel. I prefer to steer rather than just sit there while the Autohelm has all the fun, Al at times doing the navigation or on the cell phone or computer with customers. If on the phone, he would sit on the head, door closed so motor and wind noise could not be heard. Lunch or snacks any time we felt like. Discussing any topic – shoreline, things that had happened, boats or boats that were in the area. Now the food Al took care of. He had stocked the boat. Neither of us was a picky eater, but Al did like his bread. We always had bagels or fresh bread. He also likes the real peanut butter, you know, the old kind with the oil on top. Our eating was very diversified. We would have bagels and smooth peanut butter a day or two, then switch to the chunky. If in a hurry, we would wait and have egg sandwiches out in the cockpit while running, or peanut butter on a bagel. We had soups, makings for sandwiches, fresh fruit, all kinds of goodies. We never went hungry, that's for sure. *Green Dragon* is like an old pair of shoes or an old sweater to Al. Just right if chilly, just right in the heat of the day. He would move around the boat fixing a meal, checking position, keeping me in coffee, or checking the computer, at the same time checking sails. One thing just blended into the other. We were masters of our destiny.

Heading to Manchester-By-The-Sea to the Crocker Boatyard is a milk run for Al and the *Dragon*. This part of the coast is Al's backyard, from years before the *Dragon* to the present. Between conversations about maintenance, each cove or point had memories or outstanding tales for Al to tell. As for maintenance, when you own a boat this many years used as hard and as often, there's a lot of maintenance on record. Through time the *Dragon* has had frames, planking, sheer, deck, and house-side corners replaced. The original gas engine had been rebuilt and rebuilt, then replaced. Then the second one rebuilt, now the Yanmar. Previously she had a tiller that swept the cockpit. The mechanical helm is a real piece of engineering. An old truck steering box that had a 90–degree shaft was mounted above deck with the steering box mounted directly to the rudderstock. Another addition was a feathering prop, later sized for the new Yanmar. All of these discussions from one boat to another or other times. Pros and cons, makes and models. Boat talk, but in the end more and more about what immediate needs the *Dragon* has. Bottom paint, look at the prop for galvanic corrosion better known as electrolysis, that dreadful attacker of fasteners. Al knew he had struck something hard and had done some damage to the keel. Just what we would soon find out. The last time she was at Crocker's they saw a plank that had checked to the point that it should be replaced. The shipwright went digging through the reserve pile of wood. Knowing just where to look, he came up with a forty-year-old piece of mahogany stock. Milled and shaped, the *Dragon* had a fitting new plank. This is a place with craftsmanship that you read about but rarely see. We talked about replacing the fore halyards with the ones on the main and buying new ones for the main. The mains are longer so the wear would not be at the same area. Then again, both are the same age. We'll see.

The run to Manchester I had done before, but it was still interesting and fun to work the boat up-river through the rocks and moored boats. At home on the Chesapeake, we think the anchorages that we use are crowded. But here it's every time you go out. Once at Crocker's, we packed everything up for the stay at Al's. But first we had to measure the halyards. Taping a long, smaller line to the halyards, we would overhaul the halyard. Using the length of the housetop, we measured them and added more to the length for splicing. Then we re-ran the halyards. For sure, we needed to replace both.

At Al's, life was good. Phyllis made me feel at home, feeding me home cooking. Boy, Al knows just where to buy steaks just as he knows special places for bread. We indulged in evening cocktails on the patio with a pleasant view of lawn and woods while the grill got to the right temperature for the steaks. Al's had plenty to read and tours of Manchester.

While touring around Manchester getting the new line for halyards and other boat necessities, we went by Al's son Andy's house to pick up a small pump. This gave me a chance to see his wood shop and the furniture he designed and made. He has quite a collection of tools and a large workshop to work in (sure handy when you have a wood boat). Also while driving through the neighborhood, Al pointed out where he had lived and told me of how the large farms of the past are slowly being subdivided but some have held out and put the land under the protection of the community. In time, down to the boat. Using the pump from Andy's shop, Al changed the oil in the Yanmar engine and transmission and also replaced the drive belt on the Autohelm. Here again luck saved the sailor as when Al tried to purchase the new belt, he found out that they were hard to come by. Searching the Internet, he found someone who could cross-reference the numbers. We ordered two, and they were delivered right on time so the old belt could be replaced while we were still in the yard. Al checked wiring and other odds and ends such as whether the yard or he should fix the whisker stays damaged on the wild ride on the piling. Finally, we traded *Snapdragon* for an inflatable, for everything would change now. For the trek to the Chesapeake it would be better to carry the inflatable 'tween decks than to tow *Snapdragon*. Not as stylish, but safer and less trouble in open water going down the Jersey coast. Then once in Baltimore, the *Dragon* had the Great Chesapeake Schooner Race to do. Back in the yard they found no real damage to keel or forefoot from striking bottom. Painted, prop checked, tips of prop faired and adjusted, new halyards on board to run at a later time. I think we are ready to go. All of the rest of the trip I had at least been there before. But not nearly as many times as Al.

In my mind this was the halfway point of our adventure. Up until this point the weather gods had treated us very well and Neptune had not roughened the waters. Al's reading of the weather maps and predictions paid off. Each leg was pleasant and easy sailing. The course and destinations would be completely different from here on out. More open water to get to the Cape Cod Canal, Buzzard's Bay, and Long Island Sound, which have their distinct characteristics. The Hell Gate and East River would have their own challenges. Sandy Hook to Cape May, the longest open water run, then Cape May Canal and the Delaware Bay are completely different from the other bodies of water. Then one more canal, the C & D, to play with and dodge traffic. This is one of the main reasons it's much easier to have a stowed dinghy instead of towing *Snapdragon*.

Crocker's is the type of yard that I like to be in. It's an old traditional boatyard, tracks for the local trains just out front of the yard. Working lobster boats and equipment stowed around the property, vessels built of the highest quality and maintained in true Bristol fashion. Yet they have and use the most modern equipment and materials, but rightly. They know the difference between Dolfinite and the new 3M products. Remembering we're only travelers passing through, it's time to check the forecast for the time to enter the Cape Cod Canal with a favorable tide. By Al's calculations, we will be departing long before daylight.

WAYPOINT 8
L 42° 34' 16' N λ 70° 45' 26" W

"Farewell!" we cried to our dearests;
Little we cared for their tears,
"Farewell!" we cried to the humdrum
And the yoke of the hireling years;
Just like a pack of school-boys,
And the big crowd cheered us good-by.
Never were hearts so uplifted
Never were hopes so high
Robert W. Service, *Best Tales of the Yukon*

Andy dropped us off the afternoon before departure so there were no cars left in the yard. After a good night's sleep, we were ready for the challenge of going downstream in the dark of night, me on the bow with a light to watch that we did not get too close to the moored vessels. No trouble, no problem. There's something about the boat when you leave the boatyard. She feels like she's new again, clean smooth bottom, everything tight and adjusted. As the sun rose silhouetting the islands ahead of us, we were entering into a whole new day. Destination Cape Cod Canal and Buzzard's Bay. It was a flat calm day and as we motor sailed along the coast the Boston skyline could be seen and Al started to tell me tales about when he and the *Dragon* lived there.

Boston has a favorite spot in Al's heart. He has had other boats and had many memorable times, but his life changed in this old fishing port. Living next to the old fishing pier, he was able to lay the *Dragon* broadside to the wharf directly below his apartment. Fixing a light from his balcony to shine down on the boat, he was able to keep pier-side drifters from homesteading on the *Dragon*; a man has to protect his pride and joy. Then across the hall a young lady with the right cut of her jib and pleasing lines of her shear took his eye. Where else but to have the wedding aboard his other love? One became two, two became three.

The Green Dragon tavern that the boat was named after had been established in 1654 and was a favorite haunt for Paul Revere and John Hancock. Evidently the conversations for the invasion of Lexington and Concord were overheard, which made the famous ride of Paul Revere necessary, a real piece of American history. The tavern has long since been torn down and a new one has opened across the street. While investigating the tavern and its logo Al was able to find and see a picture of the dragon logo that hung over the front entrance. Now he had the artwork for his personal house flag or the ship's private signal. Here is a tale all its own. Phyllis, Al's wife and an artist in her own right, made a pennant using the old logo. Some things just take on a lifestyle all their own. Well, the pennant flew proudly from the main masthead for many a trip; then one day it got more involved in the running of the ship than it should have. Okay, here's how Al tells the tale:

"Now Steve, here's the deal. There's a PCGS mooring a ways off the shore, and we're going to pick it up under sail. No iron jib for us. The locals here won't be expecting much from a boat hailing from Boston, but when we round up smartly into this brisk breeze and scoop that mooring, we'll earn a little respect. Remember, we've got to get it on the first pass, and above all, be nonchalant. We'll drop the fore and main once we're made fast."

It was going nicely. I got the jib down at the right moment, headed up with good way on, and scandalized both peaks as we glided toward the mooring. But then it got gusty, and suddenly the wind was coming at us from all over the place. It was apparent that the foresail needed to come down right now. No problem, the halyards were laying neatly on the deck ready to run free. That is until the peak halyard block ate the tip of the house flag. It was plain to see the block had been undeterred by the dragon's fiery breath. How the Sam Hill the flag halyard got so slack I don't know, but one thing for sure, that foresail wouldn't go back up and it sure wouldn't come down. The gaff was akimbo and fore and main were both driving us again. But without that jib we had no steerage. And the outgoing tide was setting us swiftly toward one of the nearby ledges. OK. No problem. We'll just crank up the iron jib for a moment and revert to Plan B.

Steve was being nonchalant as directed. Easy for him, since he was not totally aware of the potential consequences of the unfolding situation. The old Graymarine fired right up though. Whew. But it took only a moment to wrap a pot warp around the screw. Well, that's what anchors are for, and I would have ours over in a flash. Abandoning my nonchalantness, I set about readying the anchor, which was not quite exactly ready. At that moment a lobsterman suddenly materialized off the bow.

"Appears you could use a hand," said he.

"Things have taken sort of a bad turn," said I.

"*Gets worse*," said he as he tossed a tow line.

Well, the old ragged pennant stayed home in some old forgotten place, and the *Dragon* sailed without her pennant as her punishment. But time heals all things, so Phyllis redid the pennant and house flag, having the design of the dragon somewhat different but both hand drawn and each color bright and sharp. When we arrived in Norfolk last spring to take the boat north, the first thing Al showed me was the new flags. Proud as a new father he said, "When you get time, secure the pennant to the old flag staff as the pennant is smaller then the house flag and has less windage, the larger staff is at home."

To secure the pennant I used two stainless steel cotter split rings, one through the pennant, the other through the first ring, then around the staff. This allowed the pennant to revolve three hundred and sixty degrees. Showing proper flag etiquette we had a proud ship, proud captain, and proud crew to sail off on. Not for long! After the cruise up to Washington D.C. and back in our slip in Norfolk, Al pointed out with much discomfort that the *Green Dragon* pennant had flown the coop. Sure enough it was there last night, now the only thing at the masthead was the staff. With a height of eye thirty-eight feet at the masthead, the *Dragon* had a horizon distance of seven point one nautical miles. I guess this made the old fire breather yearn to fly on the wind and travel to faraway places. The first time he only shook the halyard loose, this time he broke free from the split rings.

Now for a little trivial information. Most people do not realize that a vessel is the only place that it is proper etiquette to fly another flag higher than the American flag. It is proper to fly the Officer's flag or private signal at the masthead higher above the American flag or ensign. In nautical terms the American flag is called the ensign, which can have stars in different arrangements such as the National Merchant flag or the Yacht Ensign. The ensign is flown from the gaff peak of the main or from a halyard about the same height or if jib headed or Marconi-rigged, approximately 2/3 the length of the leach above the clew (or on a stern staff if not racing or at anchor).

As we slid down the rhumb line a gaff-rigged catboat was just about parallel and leeward of our course and moving at our speed, I sure hope she was motor sailing like us. Then to port on our weather side, we were slowly overtaking a fairly large ketch that surely was motoring. As Al talked about his life and other trips, it just seemed right to be in company of other boats; especially with a gaffer, the backdrop was perfect. Sailing in company of other boats you are always judging the other vessel and wondering her name, home port, and destination. The catboat slowly slid off to leeward on her own course to adventure. Now we had a new vessel on the horizon. Becoming larger and larger, looming up on the horizon and staying in the same position was an ocean-going tanker. As I held our course and speed the angle between us never changed, I was looking down her starboard quarter. Bearing off to port so we would pass astern and holding a line of sight of her through our starboard shrouds set us up to pass well astern, and if she had some way on she would be moving away from us. As we passed well under her stern, there was no sign of any activity or life aboard. Now looking down her port side I could see her anchor chain; this confirmed that she was lying dead in the water. I guess she was waiting for her turn to enter Boston harbor to discharge or take aboard her cargo of oil. This was the first ocean-going vessel that we had encountered, boy you just forget the size of these big boys when playing around with your kind. I guess from now on we will be dodging and standing clear of heavy commercial traffic. While all of this was going on, our air dropped even more to nothing, leaving a mirror flat sea and the only air our apparent air dead on the bow. Motoring on dropping the other traffic astern, our intention now was to pick up the entrance to the Cape Cod Canal. It looks like our speed, time, and distance calculations are right on, we feel we should arrive at the canal just as planned and at the same time as the beginning flood.

    This is the widest sea level canal in the world, first opening July 29, 1914, after the removal of thirty million cubic yards of earth. It saved a lot of time and was a lot safer than going around the Cape, but not cheaper at $16.00 a schooner for transit; back then this was stiff. Then in 1925 the government bought it and put 1400 men to work during the Depression widening and enlarging it to its present 500 feet wide by 32 feet deep. The Canal now accommodates 20,000 vessels a year.

On this day there was very little traffic, some overtaking us, one or two working against the current and passing port to port with plenty of sea room between us. It's great when everyone acts professional instead of when in a river where they feel that no one sees or cares if they obey the rules of the road or not.

Al had predicted that Buzzard's Bay would have strong headwinds against the ebbing current, making for a rough ride. Boy, was he right! As we entered Buzzard's Bay, the view forward was cornrows of whitecaps. Heading straight into them, the little Yanmar was put to the test. Smartly, we had donned foul weather gear in anticipation of a wet wild ride. Sure enough, green water was coming over the bow, running down both catwalks, sometimes as deep as the gunwales. Shedding this free, the *Dragon* rose only to take on the next oncoming wave. There's nothing to do but sit tight and take the hammering, Al at the wheel taking each sea in stride knowing the *Dragon*'s ability yet not overworking her.

For each man's hardship, the other man has pleasure. The boats sailing downwind with following seas were having the time of their life. Oh, how we wished to have that thrill and comfort while being dry. Working between them and staying clear, we finally reached a point of the rhumb line where we could bear off and reach down to the anchorage. Our turn to enjoy the weather and have an early evening sail. But then, wouldn't you know, the day was coming to an end and the wind was starting to lay down.

WAYPOINT 9
L 42° 23' 55" N   λ 76° 45' 06" W

Old boats have character
New boats do not
Old boats have stories in them
Old boats should not be forgot
    "Old Boats," Bruce Myers, *Stinkpot & Rags*

    Our destination, Marion Harbor, is rated as one of the best all-round harbors on the east coast. Because of its popularity, especially on weekends or during racing programs, it affords limited space for anchoring .Here again Al knew his way in and had planned to call the harbormaster for a mooring. Pointing out the marks and keeping us on track, we were working against a fleet of high tech racing machines heading out to the course. Most of the crews were dressed the same and colored coded to match the boat a lot like Wednesday night races at home, but more VIP, more Annapolis style. When you see crewmen wearing gloves to protect their hands, they're definitely not schooner people, real hot shots but still deck apes. Oh well, we both get the job done and both like to drive the boat to her limit.

    As we passed Bird Island Lighthouse off to starboard, there was a large very modern ketch flying a foreign flag that we could not identify. Anchored out as she was, she must have drawn a lot of water. Entering the harbor, the Beverly Yacht Club was just ahead and to starboard. This is the oldest yacht club on Buzzards Bay and supposedly one of the oldest in the country. Reciprocal privileges are welcomed, but Al felt that the far end of the club pier could be a busy place with all the racing activity; also, it is shallow. Besides, we had had a full day and had no intentions of or needs to go ashore.

The story goes that in about 1872 the Burgess Brothers, Edward and Walter, at a dinner party at their Boston home formally launched the idea of a new club to be located in the North Shore of Massachusetts Bay where their summer residence was.

Sailing regattas in this area were held by the Eastern Yacht Club in Marblehead, which refused to recognize yachts with a waterline under 30 feet. The first race held by the Beverly Yacht Club on July 13, 1872, had 10 catboats and 1 sloop. The racing circular announced a special regatta for three classes, first 21to 30 feet on the water line, second 17 feet and not over 21 feet, and boats less than 17 feet on the water line were in class three. In 1874 the Beverly Yacht Club held a union regatta off Beverly in Salem Harbor. From this it went on to provide about all of the active and official small-boat racing. This culminated in Marblehead in August 1883 when 176 boats crossed the starting line, setting a world's record that stood for 40 years. Starting off as a yacht/racing association and moving around for 23 years, for the convenience of its members it finally leased and later bought a clubhouse on Wing's Neck in 1895; its next move was to Butler Point, then to Marion. In 1955 the club bought its present location, which has quite a tale all its own. Built in 1806 and used as a ships chandlers store, servicing whalers such as the *Admiral Blake*, the last to call at Sherman's Wharf, then becoming Sherman's Inn, a stagecoach stop, then purchased by Admiral Andrew Harwood, a great grand son of Benjamin Franklin.

This little harbor holds a lot of yachting history. Edward Burgess was the leading American yacht designer in the 1880s, designing three successive America's Cup winners (in 1885 *Puritan,* 1886 *Mayflower,* and in 1887 *Volunteer*). Dying at the age of 43 at the height of his career, he had designed 207 vessels in seven years. His son, W. Starling Burgess, filled the void of his father and successfully became a world-renowned yacht designer. Following in the wake of these outstanding designers Nathanael Herrshoff became Beverly Yacht Club's first choice designer in the development of their racing yachts. In those days, the yacht club would commission a designer to design a new class boat which the club members would purchase. Out of this came such designs as the Herrshoff 15, Buzzards Bay 25, and the H12. Not to be outdone by the Burgesses, Nathanael designed American's Cup winners such as *Vigilant* 1893, *Constitution* 1901, *Reliance* 1903, and *Reliance* 1930. Carrying on this type of tradition, the club became the home club for the 1956 Olympics elimination races, first the two-person dinghies, second one-person dinghies, and the 5.5-meter races third. Does this seem like a pattern? The very first regatta had a three-class event, and now the Olympic world-class racing is a three-class affair. Another interesting piece of trivia is that Marion was the home of Captain Benjamin S. Briggs, master of the *Mary Celeste,* which was found sailing alone off the Azores without any crew or persons aboard, still the greatest sea mystery of any crew's complete disappearance.

    Boy, have I got adrift, I guess you are wondering where I'm going with all this chattering about the Beverly Yacht Club and Marion, Massachusetts. Well I guess when you're a rag man and like to sail or be around traditional vessels, you become a sort of romantic type. Just to be in company of or knowing some of the history of a place sure can whet your appetite for more knowledge. This is what I found in Judith Westlund Rosbes's book *Images of America the Beverly Yacht Club*. To me to be on an old gaffer where so much of the growth of the yachting world took place is a good feeling and fulfillment. Here we are, on a true survivor of her time and mentors.

    Owners and captains are the same as a womanizer. When entering a crowded anchorage or harbor with a forest of sticks ahead of you, a good schoonerman can pick out a pair of sticks and without being able to see the hull know right off which ones are a schooner rig like when a man walks into a crowded hall can pick out a pair of long legs with slender ankles in high heels. He knows the cut of her jib will be just right. This is how it was when we sailed into Marion Harbor. I don't know how many sailboats were moored here, but it was some forest of sticks. The moorings were laid out in squares with roadsteads between them. As we sailed down the channel I was constantly picking out the schooners. This whole harbor was full of hot racing machines and the latest designs in cruisers, but schooners held their own. About this time the harbormaster came alongside directing us to the mooring he had assigned us. Here again the harbormaster remembered the *Dragon* from her being here before and wanted to know her history and sailing background. After a long chat we assured him we were not going to go ashore, thanked him for his services, and paid up the mooring fee.

There's something about lying at anchor or hanging on a mooring at the end of the day taking in the sights just pondering over the next day's run or what should be checked on the boat. Things sure have been going smooth and every function has worked to perfection; even though you do all the right maintenance on time, things still go astray. We all have sailed on boats that just seem to have troubles. I think a lot of this is due to the cheap yachting gear that's pawned off in this day and age. So much of the gear seems to work great on weekend trips but cannot stand up to steady use as on a trip such as this. Another thing I have found is I will usually buy the next size up; say a shackle, if the manufactures chart said a 5/8 for my 28 footer I would get the next size up knowing how I work the boat. Time wears on everything, and it will fail when you need it the most because it is under its maximum load as you work in everyday sailing weather, then in heavy weather in a storm or just driving her hard you have crossed the line and are asking for failure. I know Al checks the bilge, batteries, and the running gear, and it's little things like this that sure make a trip pleasant. This gave us time to set back, have a drink, talk over the day's run, old trips, and pat ourselves on the back. There sure wasn't any reason to take a shore leave, we are quite content right here on our own little planet.

WAYPOINT 10
L 41° 46' 14" N λ 70° 45' 24" W

Sky so blue it makes you wonder
If it's heaven shining through
Earth so smiling 'way out yonder
Sun so bright it dazzles you;
Birds a-singing, flowers a-flinging
All their fragrance on the breeze;
Dancing shadows, green, still meadows—
Don't you mope, you've still got these.
                    Robert W. Service, *Best Of the Yukon*

    The next morning was picture perfect for a departure and a day of sailing, clear sky and mild sea but light air again. Once again clearing port was routine as everything went smooth and orderly. A lot of this order is because of the way the *Dragon* is kept. Everything - ship's gear, running rigging, tools, personal gear - has a home and is stowed in the proper place. If each crew member respects this system, when that 90% of boredom turns into 10% of terror the vessel can be operated with just a few commands and no loss of time rooting for gear. All lines have to be secured in their proper place, coiled and ready to run in the heat of a sail change or reduction of sail. When the skipper knows his boat and how she will handle herself if the wheel is left or how she handles on her own under certain sails and trim, he feels secure enough to move about the decks trimming or letting lines go such as when single handing. With this security he can have the crew make changes at will or sail in tight maneuvers with total control. Two can handle the *Dragon* quite easily as the purchase on all running gear is of adequate size and runs fair and clean, ground tackle secured on the foredeck ready to let go, gaskets kept handy for securing sails in a hurry. All things below are in order and kept secured; sails, extra lines, personal safety gear, and flashlights are accessible with ease day or night. This might seem normal or everyday to many readers, but after you hear the horror stories that are out there you can read between the lines and see right where all the chaos started. We all do some dumb things when not paying attention, for it is easy to daydream or just get wrapped up in other thoughts.

As we slid down Buzzards Bay and into Rhode Island Sound, there was nothing of real interest except that we were out on the water on a fine day. Al had business to conduct but he was having trouble between losing contact on the phone, trying to get e-mails out to his wife so she could make phone calls and e-mails to his customers, then they back to him. Most of the time he was in the head on the phone with the doors shut so he could hear and they had no idea just where he was. I was on my perch at the helm having the boat all to myself, not a care in the world. As we moved on down the line, we were well into Rhode Island Sound and would soon have Brenton Point off Newport abeam. Off to port on the horizon there seemed to be a large fleet or some type of regatta, some of the boats seemed to be spectators with all types of flags flying, a cluster that could be the racers, and others spread out like picket boats. Motoring on, more and more boats were coming out from Newport donned in full flag etiquette. Something important is surely going on, and this being a weekday it's not just a club regatta. My projected rhumb line had me crossing right in the middle of this fleet. Moving ahead I saw what appeared as the picket boat for the downwind mark just ahead. Knowing the concentration it takes to keep the boat moving, especially in such light air, they sure don't need to worry about my intentions. Every movement such as from crew or rudder has an adverse effect on speed and heading. As I approached the mark, I realized these were 12 meters tacking down wind. Spinnakers of all colors holding a good shape and being worked as the light air shifted from side to side. Seeing the picket boat I dipped my starboard bow and fell off to show him I would stay clear, acknowledging my intent by not starting to head me off, I stayed on this new course. Now a third dimension came on the scene: a helicopter started to circle overhead, I'm sure filming the event. First he was up wind going from side to side, then turning to get side shoots, swinging around coming down wind, moving from boat to boat getting the right angle and background. At times it seemed that he was trying to use us as part of the background. He would be low, swing around, then raising up fast and spinning around, then dropping down, all the time making sure his prop wash had no effect on the fleet. Calling Al to see this show as it unfolded and watching out so not to get in their way I did not realize he couldn't hear me because of being in the head on the phone. The fleet was closing in on me, so again I dipped the bow to starboard away from them and they held their course jockeying for a better position, each trying to gain the lead and stay in good air, clear of the boat astern and his foul air. The decks were lined with crew; it looked like at least fifteen. Each time I felt they needed more room ahead I would steer clear. Never did anyone try to divert me, and the racers held steady on their course. As the fleet crossed our track astern, I could bring the head up and finally be back on my original course. Feeling good about the way they let me cruise through the course and get a grand view of 12 meters racing, I felt I had handled the rules of the road proper and always kept downwind. Being a racer and past foredecker, all-around crewmember, and navigator gave me the advantage of seeing it from their point of view. Back on course and them well astern, Al came on deck.

"What's that all about?"

"Man you should have seen it, I called you when it all started. It was a three-ring circus. First ring had the spectator's fleet, ring two the racers, and ring three the helicopter."

"Did you have to change course to give them room?"

"Oh yeah, I had to work through the whole mess but no one seemed to mind, not a single picket boat moved off station."

What a day, for one that started off much as the others it sure became very interesting without a Chinese fire drill or an unwanted major change in the weather. But Point Judith is still ahead, and nothing should be taken for granted. I have passed Point Judith several times, but never in the harbor. Knowing it is the ferry terminal for the Block Island ferry and the home port for a major fishing fleet with a history of groundings, we might just see a lot of action.

WAYPOINT 11
L 41° 22' 03" N λ 71° 12' 27" W

And now that we are landed where the rum is mighty cheap,
We'll drink success to the cap'n for guidin' us o'er the deep
A health to all our sweethearts, an' to our wives so fair
Not another ship could make that trip but *Balena* I declare.

"Dundee Whalers," Stan Hugill, *The Bosun's Locker*

Sometimes too much information is too much. Reading, approaching is quite dangerous due to a treacherous ledge. Then in the *Cruising Guide* it mentions to stand off at least 2 miles from Point Judith as the waters are thriving with fish traps. All of this if you are approaching from the northeast, that's us. This is the entrance to Narragansett Bay and the Point is like a finger, or as they say a Nag's Head, pointing out more then a mile from the Rhode Island coast. As it was, the weather held with no traffic, so going in was a piece of cake. If the wind had been up, rail down, and a sea running, the plotter would have been a godsend. Our eyes would have been glued on it, watching the depths and contour of the bottom for the ledges. In the old days they depended on the lighthouses, taking bearings for distance off; the lead line is of no use while moving in these conditions. This is the reason for of all the groundings. On a day like this you can more or less sail by the seat of your pants. Moving forward the marks were easily picked up, and we entered with no other vessels and I had time do some sight seeing as Al talked me in. Entering, you have a breakwater to starboard for the outside anchorage and a sea wall to port as you enter the harbor. Moving along to port there is an opening for the south entrance. At this junction you follow the channel on in. We motored up to the fuel dock, fueled up, got ice, then moved to another floating dock, laid-up alongside for the night, fenders down, springs fore and aft. We felt secure. Al went up the pier to pay up, find the showers, and check out restaurants. Returning he said we were in luck - David Clarke off the *Winfield Lash* was here, the *Winfield* was up on the hard having her bottom and topsides done. He had a car and we could all go to dinner at one of the local spots. The *Winfield Lash* is the schooner we rendezvoused with off Sandy Hook, New York, last spring on our way to Mystic. After a shower and looking over the *Winfield*, we were off to George's Restaurant, a local spot where the genuine fishermen and tourists like us hang out. David asked how long had we been out and when did we expect to reach Baltimore. Both laughing, Oh, in about a week or so, it depends. Then the conversation went to how nice it was to just cruise, not like delivering where time is money, money at the owner's expense. We all agreed this way you get to know the ports and anchorages, with time to read up on the location and talk to the locals. Hey, don't forget the restaurants, man, we sure do eat well. Eating, drinking, and swapping tales made a very pleasant evening pass on faster than we realized. Back at the marina we stood on the upper deck and talked some more, it was just too nice of a night to turn in.

 About an hour or so after we left Point Judith, the air started to rise and set up a fair sea as we had the current with us and the wind ahead. Our destination was Dutch Wharf Boat Yard Marina in Branford, Connecticut. To get there we would pass through The Race, the narrowest part of the east end of Long Island Sound. I had journeyed through here a few years ago after visiting Block Island on our way to Mystic. We had been told that at maximum ebb and no wind the water is forced up from the bottom, which is very uneven with pot holes, making the water shoot up to the surface forming mushroom like domes on the surface. As planned, we hit The Race with the maximum ebb in a dead calm, and sure enough, we were fascinated and spent some time motoring around in the distortion of water. Now Al was going to work his way through Watch Hill Passage more on the north side between Watch Hill on the north shore and Fishers Island, which would make a shorter passage. The Cruising Guide alerts you of the sideways set of strong current, southward on the ebb northward on the flood, at times strong enough for the buoys being towed under and you can inadvertently be swept onto the rocks or reefs. We had a fair amount of current, but not like out in the middle between Fishers Island and Plum Island.

There was quite a bit of traffic, sail, and power going in all directions. Sailing with a good heel, bow dipping to the oncoming waves but not shipping water like back in Buzzards Bay was a great feeling. Laying a line between the marks and giving way to the privileged vessels and staying in the channel all the time keeping way on was fun. Here again the boats sailing east on the wind were having the time of their life, I'm sure. We had been yearning for a ride just like this for quite awhile. Working on down the sound it opened up to where we were in the full width of the sound so traffic was not as concentrated, allowing us to hold a longer lay line and less tacking. But as the day passed on, so did the wind until the old Yammey was the only driving force. About this time we were entering a large shallow bay, but heading for the Big and Little Mermaids, two islands you bring close aboard, then swing hard to starboard. Now Al warned me the channel is only about 100 feet wide and gets narrower as you go up, with only about 8 feet of water. Sure enough, it got narrower with stakes on starboard side spaced so boats could be moored fore and aft along the shore but could not swing into the channel. Looking ahead there was a very large modern marina full of white shiny powerboats but the river turned to port and the shore line became pristine but narrower, and ahead was another bend to starboard. When Al had called ahead to arrange a slip, they had informed him that they had one but closed at 5:00. The river looked like it was running out of length and us out of time. Turning to starboard Al called again telling them our position, they in turn said we only had one more bend and we would see them and they were waiting. Ah, there they were, standing at the end of the travel lift dock. When they saw the *Dragon,* they signaled us to lay her alongside. Checking out the situation, the width of the channel (which was not much), and boats moored right across from the dock Al felt it better to lay stern- to for convenience in the morning when departing

After seeing the *Dragon* no way were they going to put her in the intended slip, no sir, keep her right here. Boy, we were sure in wood boat heaven. Across from us were some wooden sloops, two schooners, and a couple of powerboats. Next to us and along the dock were more wooden powerboats. We were told that they do the most maintenance and refinishing on wood boats in the area. Al can sure pick the out-of-the-way places. The modern marina might have a swimming pool and restaurant and the Branford Yacht Cub might have reciprocal privileges, but for these two old codgers this was home. After walking around the marina we went off to find the pizza shop in town. After a good night of sleep, up early and downriver heading for City Island, a port that Al liked and that had many tales to tell was at the end of our day's run.

Leaving The Mermaids this time to starboard, out of the bay area we were once more westward bound on Long Island Sound. Not the air and sea we had yesterday but motor sailing right along, at this point in life you appreciate any comfort you get. Nearing the narrow western end of the Sound we were in the vicinity of Sands Point and once again on a collision course with the weather mark of a regatta. Definitely not 12 meters but racers just the same. Seeing the picket boat standing off the mark I headed to keep her off my starboard, keeping clear of every one. Here again no one signaled us to give more way. Watching the racers tacking up to the mark, rounding, setting their spinnakers, and laying a new course was strange. Some seemed to do a 180, others fell way off like on a reach. Then it became clear, two or more classes were racing with a command mark. As we sailed down the rhumb line we encountered more and more traffic going in all directions, small, big, power or sail they all seemed crowded and in a hurry, changing course and speed, making crazy wakes off each other's wakes. Oh, it's Sunday. Old goats like us know the time of tide, current, and sunset, not the day of the week. Come on, they just run together. Our course now lay along the south shore of Long Island, but if we held our course we would work up to the north shore near Execution Rocks lighthouse.

We were not too far from City Island, our port of call, but in a lot of traffic, pleasure and commercial. If commercial, I am the burdened vessel without doubt; if the other is a pleasure boat, I always figure the other guy doesn't know the rules of the road so I am more on guard and ready to divert from my regular intention. Then again every time two boats are abreast a race is on, no way is a captain going to let the other point higher, sail faster, sure enough not to be overtaken on the leeward side. This is sailing whether racing, coursing, or just out playing boats.

This was a very pleasant passage after all as every one gave way or steered around each other keeping clear but passing close aboard, each in turn giving the high sign, everyone out for the day and taking in all the sights. It's great how people will just wave to each other as they pass or cross tacks. I guess it's an old holdover from the true days of sail when a ship was raised on the horizon, maybe the last one seen was weeks or months ago. If by chance they could hail each other by voice or flags they would exchange positions, time, and times from the last port of call. Whaling ships would haul up close to each other, backwind sails, and have a gamming session. The long boats would be put over and the crew could go over to the other vessel and socialize, exchange mail if the other vessel was heading home or at least be home before them. Captains could compare notes, check positions, swap supplies, sometimes pass over barrels of oil to be sent home so he could stay out longer, and refill her bilges. All of this activity and the weather being just right for sailing sure made for a fulfilling day.

WAYPOINT 12
L 41° 23' 11" N   λ 71° 30' 58" W

> as down the Mersey we set sail, to New York we wus bound,
> this poor young lad began to think of his friends he'd left behind;
> this poor young lad began to think of his friends and his native shore,
> and he cursed the day he'd stowed away in the *City of Baltimore*
>
> "*City of Baltimore*," Stan Hugill, *The Bosun's Locker*

Now everything would change. We were sailing in the west end of Long Island Sound. Our westward passage through Long Island Sound had taken us through suburban and rural areas having lots of land and open spaces making a pretty shoreline and plenty of sea room for maneuvering around vessels. But this would all change after leaving City Island. City Island is considered the first New England town when going north even though it is not actually in New England. Because of its country appearance and small town life style it has the flavor and the quaintness of any New England town. Now sailing west of City Island we would be right in the metropolis of Manhattan Island, close quarters, heavy commercial traffic, tugs, barges, ships, private yachts, high speed ferries, and commuter planes landing on the East River. Shortly after entering the East River, we will pass between Rikers Island and La Guardia Airport with its runway right up to the water's edge, which is the channel. Now we all know the story about how some of the planes don't get airborne at take off and become vessels until they settle to the bottom. With all of this, the shoreline will become very commercial, dirty, and drab. But first we have to continue on to City Island, which is just ahead around Hart Island. City Island is surrounded by Long Island Sound and Eastchester Bay. Coming from the northeast you will pass Execution Light, from the south Stepping Stones light.

Holding our course we were able to leave Hart Island to starboard, passing around the west end, then going north to Consolidated Yachts boat yard located on the south side of the City Island. Approaching the boat yard, we had an anchorage to starboard and an anchored barge ahead. Clearing the barge, which is the breakwater for the yard, was a set of piers leading to the far end of the yard. All the piers were floating but old and not in the best condition, each secured to each other with a board between them so you didn't step in the space between them. All of this generated quite a noise from the movement of the wave action. When we first entered we motored up between the first set of piers, not knowing for sure which slip to use. Nearly at the head of the fairway we came about to go out when some other boaters pointed to another slip, but Al continued out and around to the other set of slips feeling we would get more protection and it would be easier to cast off our lines when leaving. After securing the boat, Al went up the pier to talk to Mr. Wesley Rodstom, the yard manager. With a big smile on, he said we could move the boat up to the travel-lift slip and lay at the end of the pier where the ramp to the floating piers was. Mr. Wesley remembered the *Dragon* and Al from last year and felt she would do just fine there and if she needed to be moved so they could use the travel-lift, we would be around to move her.

Walking up the ramp put us right in one of the world's leading yachting centers, often referred to as New York's headquarters for yacht building and repair. A place we have all read about and would love to roam around in if you were interested in the America's Cup races or other classic boats.

The Minneford Boat Yard, which built 12-meter yachts such as *Columbia* (1958), *Constellation* (1964), *Intrepid* (1967), *Courageous* (1974), and *Freedom* (1980), is right next door to Consolidated Yachts just for starters. This island is only 1.5 miles long and has only one main street, City Island Ave., which has most of the restaurants and other businesses. At home we feel that Annapolis, Maryland, is the sailing center and big time. In City Island within walking distance there are four yacht clubs, seven marinas, and six or more full-service yacht yards, two sail makers, one of which is Ulmer-Kolius; all with full services from building to major changes to general maintenance and fast, reliable service for transit vessels; and the Island is home port to nearly 2,000 boats. All of this and it is part of the borough of Bronx, yes, Bronx of New York City.

WAYPOINT 13
L 40° 52' 59" N λ 73° 43' 04" W

> And now we're anchored in the Bay with the Kanakas all around,
> Whit chants and soft alohas they greet us homeward bound;
> And now ashore we'll have good fun and paint them beaches red,
> Awaking in the arms of an island maid, with a big fat achin' head
>
> "Rolling Down To Old Maui", Stan Hugill, *The Bosun's Locker*

The marina sits high above the floating piers, during high water it is about ten to twelve feet, and with a seven and a half foot tide range at low water it makes the travel-lift pit look very large and deep – also, the ramp up can be quite steep. Going up the steep ramp not only takes you to high ground but this could be the highlight of the trip. All along this trip Al has talked or referred to City Island as one of his best ports. We would eat in the Tree House and meet the regulars that hang out there such as the old man that had dinner every night at the same table. Us calling him old! But first the boat had to be secured and put to sleep. The forecast had predicted rain, so slickers on, off we went for some shore duty. After climbing the ramp to the top, you could really see the size of the yard, mostly a powerboat yard but some interesting sail and old workboats stored about. There was a very large building I'm sure was for winter storage and a place to work in out of the weather. This is one spot I will surely check out tomorrow when rummaging around. Now the yard was just one property in from City Island Av. and west of the main part of the business area. Walking along you sure felt like you were in a small waterfront town, lawns and grass between the sidewalk and the curb, old style telephone poles with the red call boxes used back when by the fire and police departments. School 175 has half of a dory on the wall and a modern sculpture or model of the ship of the first Dutch explorer that landed on City Island. Further on we passed an old store that was a secondhand or junk shop that had anything nautical, really anything old and discarded but one place for sure I will visit. The trees in this block had old veins all twisted and burley hanging from them, really the perfect setting for the store. Finally in the block of the Tree House was the Black Whale restaurant, the diner, and in the next block or so were the Crab house and an outdoor ice cream garden.

 Strolling along without a care in the world, taking in all the sights, made this trip so different from a delivery job. Time is our call, and we can say we will check this or that out tomorrow or stop and satisfy our curiosity. No in and out of port after refueling and stocking up on ships stores as when sailing on a paycheck.

 Approaching the Tree House and seeing the men sitting at tables along the sidewalk gave us the feeling that we were in Europe, maybe because I knew it was an Albanian establishment. Entering the restaurant the first thing I noticed was how small it was inside, walking to the back the bar was to the right and small tables to the left, and sure enough the old man was having dinner. Al immediately introduced me to the elderly gentleman as Mr. Kirk Boyce. Such formality – "Mr. Kirk Boyce" – just didn't sound right. Here is a gentleman with his own charisma because of his age, appearance, and past experiences. It just seems right and proper to still refer to him as 'the old man.' As we bellied up to the bar, which was also very small and compact, we could see a tree in a glass enclosure going from floor to ceiling, and there appeared to be a courtyard further back. Everyone knew Al, handshakes all around, big smiles, then the owner ordering drinks to be set up. Al was back, stories to be told of where has he been and where was he going. Oh, but a new waitress named Mimosa has been hired and what a knockout, new to this country and not used to our slang. We were off to one helluva evening having fun with the use of words and slang. It sure was going to lead to a very interesting night.

First, we told the attending bartender that we wished that all our drinks be made by Mimosa. The bartender really didn't take to this lightly, but he was willing to show Mimosa how to mix each drink and show her the chemistry of each drink such as a martini or the difference between a rail rum on the rocks or top shelf rum on the rocks. Each time she made a different drink he showed her which glass or tumbler to use. She was having as much fun as we were and getting on the job training.

Mimosa is one fine looking young lady, very pretty eyes that you just have to look into when talking to her, a great smile with natural white teeth. It was fun joking with her and trying to keep her attention but not confuse her too much with all the questions we were firing at her.

Most of the time she was too short to reach the overhead glasses or the type of liquor on the top shelf that we were ordering. Trying to cover my bases, I explained to the bartender that by her learning her way around the bar she'd be a big help when it was crowded with drinks being ordered one behind the other. This seemed to settle the water, but you could see he still had dark clouds in his vision. Oh well, the fun had started and now the old man had also bellied up to the bar to join in the fun.

About this time I noticed that the men who had been outside had come in. One or two were standing at the far end of the room by the courtyard, the other one between us and the front door. Now each one seemed to be interested in the joking and fast talk, but then again they seemed to play the part of the pawn in a chess game protecting the queen. For sure this was no waterfront bar or New Jersey mob hangout, but being from Baltimore and a real seaport my guard was up and well aware of my surroundings. Maybe I was overreacting, but the only two ways out were blocked and this was their turf and they sure were not going to let some stumblebum hit on their queen. One thing for sure, Al is a well-respected gentleman and I had come in under tow with him. I'm sure Al took no notice. To them we were surely not fishermen or merchant seamen so in their culture our tales of roaming from place to place made us look like sea gypsies. But it only took one eye contact from the owner, and they were at ease. As the night went on and over dinner, the conversations went around to the past of City Island and the part it played in the building of wartime vessels and the part the old man played. Getting close to closing time, we asked if we could buy a loaf of bread to take back, then ordered a round of Grand Marnier. As Mimosa poured it out she was sure giving us a full amount, whoa, whoa, take it easy, that stuff is expensive, you do not pour it out like the other liquors. Then when she brought the bread she had wrapped it in so much aluminum foil that the foil cost more than the bread. Showing our concern, we tried to explain the difference and that she was too generous; the owner just smiled and took it in stride. Saying our goodnights, out into a light rain we headed back feeling good, laughing about how things had gone. Slowly we started to talk about what had to be done tomorrow on the boat and that we should get an early start as rain was predicted for the next couple of days.

WAYPOINT 14
L 40° 50' 29" N λ 73° 46' 54" W

I wish I wuz in the 'Jolly Sailor'
Along wid Irish Kate a-drinkin' beer',
An' them I thought what jolly chaps were sailors
An' with me flipper I wiped away tear.

"Paddy Lay Back," Stan Hugill, *The Bosn's Locker*

Waking up after a night under the leaking deck, I was well informed that it had rained harder later in the night and some of the work planned for the day would be put on hold. Once up I realized Al had gone ashore, probably to the diner to rendezvous with the old man. The walk up to the diner did my knee good as I had been curled up throughout the night to find a dry spot; life in the forepeak, hey, that would be a good title for a book. Sure enough, they were at the counter and well into coffee and bagels but no peanut butter - that's saved for when under way. Comparing notes on last night's adventure with the towels, leaks, and the condition of our sleeping bags over a cup of hot coffee was surely not as bad as living it. Al had some leakage over his bunk but not as bad as usual. It seems that when the boat is setting still the water finds its way to lower levels and you can live in a dry place once found. But when under way it runs all over the place and has you trying to find high ground. The old man had worked the waterfront all his life and sure knew what we were talking about, been there done that. As he heard our tale of woe you could see it brought back memories and a kind of smile that showed he was sure glad it was in the past, no desire to go back in time. At that time work on the waterfront used labor intense equipment and was usually on a tight time schedule regardless of weather. For him it surely was not play like it is for us, but you could see he felt a great satisfaction in being part of it. He had lived through the Depression when you had to out wit, out work, and out perform the next guy for every job. Then came along World War II with more work than you wanted, long hours, pushing seven days straight with no time off. Short on manpower and material but a necessity to keep the wartime machine going full force. Hard times, hard work makes a hard man.

Strolling back to the boat in no real hurry gave me time to check out the hardware store and junk shop. It's nice to just roam around and window shop, you just might find something for the boat, something you need but had no idea where to find it. Back in the boat yard I checked out the showers, then started to nose around checking out the types and condition of the boats stored here. Working my way over to the big storage building, I found an old open workboat in very poor shape, but I'm sure they just didn't have the heart to break her up. Finding the door to enter the storage building I went inside, boy, what a find. It had two or three big power boats in the back, one being worked on, an R.V. camper, old marine engines, a car or two, and miscellaneous equipment. Best of all there was a street rod, an open wheel channeled roadster right out of the '50s, further back a restored '50s Ford pickup, next to it a restored Willy's Jeep pickup. Here the whole hot rod movement was represented. The roadster, the real street racer, driven by a car head with one hand on the wheel, the other on the floor shifter, and an eye on the red light, engine with rpm's up ready for the light to change. Pop the clutch, bang, shift to second, and off the line. The Ford pickup would be used for cruising around picking up chicks, then off to the drive-in for a hamburger, fries and a milk shake, all delivered by a car hop on roller skates. Lined up with other street rods and all with the same radio station on, tuned to the Wolfman. Now the Willy's, not really a hot rod but a car of the time. Every surfer's dream was to have a woody or a Jeep. She would have been driven by a tanned sun-bleached hair jock always in company with his first love, his board. If the Jeep was restored like this one, the surfer was a weekend warrior with Daddy's Jeep. If an old rusted rattletrap, then here was a true high wave surfer on a low income. Youth is wasted on the young. First I had to find Mr. Wesley and find out if these were his, then off to show Al. Back outside I came face to face with the old workboat, it was like the old man. Here outside where it had spent its life always at hard work, dependable and abused but the moneymaker. The men that manned her had dirt under their fingernails, work-worn clothes, black dirt creases in their hands, but proud. Not like those money pits, the pleasure boats and toy cars kept inside.

Talking to Mr. Wesley I found out that the cars belonged to his partner, who had the body shop on the City Island Avenue side of the property. But the Willy's was his; he had several when in another time and life as a surfer out in California. Rusted away by salt spray and the ocean environment meant that they had to be replaced and most likely when found were not too much better. In later years he found this one in one of the northwestern states in good shape because of the dry climate. Restored to like new it gave him back a piece of his youth. I guess that's why Al and I are out playing with boats, we are just not ready to swallow the anchor. Finding Al on the boat at the laptop surfing out in cyber space, getting the latest poop and weather conditions with a coffee cup in hand, he was in his environment. I asked if he wanted to step back in time. Off to the shed. Once inside Al saw a large mast along the wall, it must have been at least a foot across at the heel and eighty feet long. All standing rigging, turnbuckles, cleats, and gooseneck still on. Later we found out from Mr. Wesley that he had the other mast from a schooner out in the mast loft. Both were offered to anyone who could use and remove them. You just don't know what you will find.

The light rain had stopped but it was still overcast so it was wise to wear our slickers as we would be on the go 'til late. First we thought we would walk up to the museum, then off to the Harlem Yacht Club, then heading back to the boat we would pass the Tree House for dinner and a night cap. While we were walking along, a car pulled over close to the curb and the woman driving was trying to get our attention. Moving closer to the car so I could hear her, the first thing I noticed was the inside of the car looked like Fibber McGee's closet, a real mess. Surely no room if she was to offer a ride, maybe she wanted directions. She started out introducing herself as the crazy cat lady, explaining that she fed all the homeless cats but the community was not impressed. It seemed the residents on the streets she patrolled would chase her away. Then she went on about a male friend, friend only, after all she was a church person and only doing a kind thing. After telling her we were just out for a walk, she said she would see us later if she wasn't chased off. Ok, because of our yellow slickers I guess to her we looked like Sargasso weed washed up on shore, harmless, not chasers of cat feeders. I know a friend in need is a friend indeed, but I don't want a damn cat to feed. Walking away, we had a good laugh. Finding the City Island Historical Society / Nautical Museum, which is housed in the old Public School #17, was no trouble. After all, we are navigators and this is a small town - but it has a cat welfare department.

    Once inside the museum, back to serious behavior. Going through the different rooms seeing the memorabilia, photographs, models, and a room just the way it would have been in the old school days, I was most impressed with the World War II photos. City Island railways were one busy place, and wood was still the major building material. Craftsmen who built the high dollar yachts must have had a heyday with the fast construction system where the joints were filled with filler and the gray paint hides everything, no varnish. As I roamed around I found Al talking to one of the volunteers, and sure enough he knew someone who was an acquaintance of a friend who belonged to some other organization. Sure enough they looked into the organization's register and found the person; you can run but not hide. It was closing time and the volunteers were ready to call it a day, and for us the sun was over the yardarm, time for the day's share of grog. On the course plotted for the day, the Harlem Yacht Club was our next port of call.

As you walk through the yacht club, the walls are lined with past line officers dating back to the eighteen hundreds. Yes, the club started in Harlem in 1883, and then bought property here in City Island, which was called a station; for ten years they had both locations. Then in 1894, a Victorian style clubhouse was built but lost in a fire. In 1915 this present building took its place. Being accessible to the Sound, it is in an ideal location. As the locals say, it has a sizeable contingent of New Jerseyans and Manhattanites. Sitting at the bar you had a panoramic view of the slips and moorings. Although it was shallow, there seemed to be a fair amount of good-sized boats. At first I thought it had a powerboat majority but found out it is 80% sail to 20% power. In the eighteen hundreds yachting was predominantly sail. During the '20s and '30s, motor vessels were just coming on the scene. After World War II it turned basically into a powerboat club.

Because of the advanced development of hulls and power plants, powerboats were very dependable and economically feasible. The power boating industry started to show the wife and children involved in boating in their ads, making it more a family involvement. The new concept of interior design being more commodious with added luxuries got the wife's attention. This brought about the increase in the majority of registered boats and membership with power vessels. Sailboat design had not changed in design or accommodations since the prewar boats. This all changed for the sailor with the development of space age material such as fiberglass and Dacron, giving a better performing and a more spacious accommodating boat for the buck. A molded hull having no need for frames, ceiling, knees, or other interior construction gives a lot more space. In later years, because of the sailing programs and promoting regattas, sail has made a great comeback. Their racing schedule is quite full; they have round-the-buoy, overnight, J24 one-design, and the Vice Commodore's Regatta in which the crew have to be non-sailors. Last summer the schooner *Delight* from Cape Charles VA., owned and skippered by Tim Callis, stopped off here for a few days. He received a lot more hospitality than just reciprocal privileges, so he invited the line officers for a sail. While sailing through the anchorage they were waving and yelling to other members, taking them by surprise, possibly because the line officers are stout power boaters.

The social atmosphere at the bar was low key, small talk in low tones by the members, not the hustle-bustle as if a regatta or other social event were in progress. Very upscale. No one asked if we belonged to another yacht club or not, I guess we just looked the part. It seems schooner men are not yachters; we seem to hang on to the old blue-collar attitude, talking together and enjoying each other's company without all the regimentation or diplomatic etiquette. While we were having small talk with the barmaid about the club and neighborhood, more and more members were arriving dressed in coats and ties. Realizing it was eight bells or 4:00, dinnertime, we decided to get back on course for the Tree House, our next watering hole.

At the end of the parking lot the property next to the club's property had the neatest house tucked away in between an overgrown growth of trees, flower beds covering the grass lawn, and shrubbery hiding most of a bay window and the front door, painted in pastels of a light gray blue on the cedar shake shingles, a darker blue gray on the window and door frames, shutters, and flower boxes. It's hard to explain the design; it definitely did not belong to this area. A gingerbread decoration along the roof eves made us wonder if a cuckoo clock bird came out and whistled the time; we would not be surprised. Out came Al's cell phone: I have to send a picture of this to Denise and tell her you just bought a house.

WAYPOINT 15
L 40° 50' 29" N λ 73° 46' 54" W

An' now we've arrived in Bramley Moor Dock
An' all of them flash judies on the pier head do flock;
The barrel's run dry an' our five quid advance
An'l guess it's high time for to git up an' dance
> *The Bosun's Locker*, Stan Hugill

Looking down the street, I caught the crazy lady's car crossing the intersection from starboard to port. She had gotten in under the radar to feed her dependents; waving, she stayed her course and made her getaway. Smiling, I told Al that if she showed up again it was his turn to talk to her and he would see I was not exaggerating. As we walked along Al said that he had had some minor surgery to his leg when last home and it was time to have the stitches removed. No trouble, I had noticed a clinic on the avenue in one of the blocks near the Tree House and we could find it tomorrow.

Entering the Tree House the first thing I noticed was that there were a lot more customers than the night before. As we entered the bar area, sure enough the old man was having dinner. Letting Al have the first seat open at the bar I was able to take the seat on the corner, which I prefer. If possible I always sit here because you have command of both sides. On one side, you see behind the bar as well as the faces of the customers or the bartender's view. The next thing I noticed was Mimosa was more involved working behind the bar. Sitting in the first seat at the bar was a lady of color having a conversation with the bartender. After introductions all around, we were told that they are both actors and have been in several plays together. Hearing them talk about the life of an actor, the fast pace of life in New York City, and the constant searching for work sure did not appeal to me.

Comparing notes, they discussed the types of work and rates of pay and different directors. The bar job was to satisfy hunger and the need for shelter. Knowing our way of life, I felt they were jealous and I tried to explain that we had gone through the same growing pains of life. The dark side of our life style is it is the last hurrah, old age is in the wings readying for the last act. Having finished dinner and seeing an open spot at the bar, the old man rafted up alongside Al. Hearing the conversation the old man started telling us how all the equipment he had had had been steam powered. That meant it had to be fired up to have steam enough to operate long before the crew was on the job. Summer or winter, snow or ice, rain or shine. How he had to recover his anchor after a storm that had been fouled by someone else's abandoned barge, a lot of extra work after a full day. After recovering the anchor, he took the barge in tow and ended up with one more barge in the fleet. At times like this, life looks stacked up against you. Returning from the pump out station, I saw Mimosa had come around on our side of the bar and was standing where I had been sitting. She was looking over the shoulder of the man next to my seat, who was showing her a video of some CD on his laptop. Seeing I had returned he turned the laptop so I could see, saying she is amazed at the amount of music that is available in this country. Introducing himself as Mark Head, Dr. Mark Head, I immediately turned to Al; we have a doctor in the house! Why, do you guys need one? In a way, Al has stitches in his leg and they are due to come out. Here let me see, put your leg up on the stool so I can see. Pulling up his pants leg while lifting his leg for Doc to see, while everyone else at the bar turned to see. Doc. asked for a flashlight, scissors, and tweezers. The bartender handed him a flashlight. The owner returned with his wife's eyebrow set. Then the doctor was handed a jigger of some type of high-end liquor. The liquor poured on first, then the stitches extracted, job complete, remainder of liquor poured into Doc's remaining wine.

From here the conversations went everywhere, and after each story Mark would make a statement if it was right or not - he had already looked it up on the computer during the conversation. Some vessel would be mentioned that had been built here in City Island and the old man knew her name, date of construction and who skippered her. Mark would follow up with the owner's name and how he acquired his wealth such as if he were a railroad or steel baron. Somehow the conversation got around to how the word SHIT came about. Al explained that back when there was an abundance of manure and not enough fertilizer, the manure would be bundled in gunnysacks and shipped wherever needed. While in the cargo hole of the ship it would become wet from sloshing bilge water and ferment. Not only did it stink, but the methane gas given off was highly explosive. So sailors, not being the best spellers, would print S.H.I,T. meaning S-ship H-high I-in T-transit. This would mean that the bundles would be stacked high enough on other cargo so that bilge water did not reach them. Right off the bat Mark came back with the *OED* version of the story, which referred to this origin but didn't necessarily confirm it – but it sounds good at the bar. What a tool to have at a bar, if you tell a tale it better be right, no bullshit here no matter how you spell it.

Realizing it was eight bells, midnight bar time, and not wanting to turn into a pumpkin but only into our bunks, we said our farewells. It had stopped raining earlier in the day so on the way back to the boat we again discussed the work on the boat to be done; first I had to replace the halyards for the run down the New Jerry coast.

Rising to a pretty day I had an early breakfast in the diner, then back to the boat. We have been asked more then once if all the ropes and lines in the rigging are used. Believe me, every single one has a job. A true traditionally rigged gaffer's running rigging uses three to four times more line then a modern Marconi rigged vessel. A Marconi main or any mast supported Marconi sail has just a two part halyard, which is only twice the length of the height of the mast. It also rides in a cove in the mast and boom or rides on a track not laced to the spar as a traditional rig. Mechanical advantage on a modern rig for tension is gained by the use of a winch. Now a gaff sail has a spar called a gaff boom to support the top length of the sail, which is laced on, then the luff edge is laced to the mast. Here again if the sail is laced on by lacing it around and around the spar, it will allow the sail to move along the spar and have the greatest stretch and sag in the middle. It should be laced properly with a running hitch that will hold the sail firmly at each grommet to prevent it from slipping. The foot is also laced to the boom. This takes a lot more length of line than the total length along the sail because of the wraps and hitches around the spars. To hoist the sail takes two halyards: the throat and the peak that are raised together, and then the peak, which is raised higher to trim. First, the throat halyard is a three- or four- part tackle, which means the running parts are three to four times longer then the height of the mast they are serving. The peak halyard passes through at least three blocks, first to a block on the mast, second to a bridle located in the middle of the gaff boom, then third back to a block on the mast higher than the first, then out to the peak or end of the gaff boom. All of this just for sails flown from a mast. To apply tension, the haul end goes around a belaying pin and is then sweated up, no winches here, only labor. Jibs have downhauls because of being tacked to the most forward end of the bowsprit, or widow maker as called by old fishermen. I could go on and on and on about the use of lines not found on modern rigged vessels. The *Green Dragon* is a petite little lady with only enough standing and running rigging to do the job. Being baldheaded fore and aft, she has no running rigging for topsails or need for running backstays. They say give a man enough rope and he will hang himself, and I am not about to do that.

To rerun the halyards, you take one end of the new line and secure it to the haul end of the old halyard. The old halyard is pulled out through the set of blocks, hauling the new line through them. When completed, the new line is spliced to the becket on the block, making the line now a halyard. I usually do the throat halyard first. Then I run the other end of the new line through the peak halyard system, splicing the standing part to the gaff. Now this means that the one line is both halyards. With the gaff laying on the main boom it uses the full length of each halyard, so the tail or remaining part of each halyard can be cut to the right length. Cutting the single line and whipping the ends turns it into two separate halyards. To start, I first looked for a needle so I could whip the two lines together, only to find the only needles were too small and rusty. My next choice was to tape them together; completing this, I was ready to start. Hauling on the old halyard until it got to the first sheave in the block I felt some tension, giving a little tug I saw to my horror the new line falling to the deck at the same rate as the old one. Shit, this is the worst thing that can happen to a rigger. Like a whipped pup I went with my tail between my legs to find Al. Explaining my predicament and the need for suggestions was not easy. Looking at the two ends, my mistake was taping the lines together. Making the tape tight I had squeezed out water from inside the line, preventing the sticky stuff from sticking. Off to the sail maker up the road for some needles. Now to reeve the line through the channel of the block secured up on the mast. Al suggested he could use the bosun's chair on a halyard higher up, if I could haul him up. This is really my job, but I weigh more then Al. Before my knee replacement I could have shinnied up, but that was then, this is now. Checking the lead for the tail of the halyard to the sheet winch, we saw we needed a turning block rigged at the base of the mast. Blocks are one thing a schooner has plenty of, muscle power from crew is another thing. As I started to winch him up I heard someone coming down the ramp to the pier and looking up, it was no one else other then Dr. Mark Head. He looked like Paul Bunyan, big and all muscle. Not giving him a chance to say hi, I told him a doctor is just what we needed. Now in the movies the man of the house is sent out for hot water when the doctor arrives, but here the captain of the boat is sent aloft. Explaining our project and showing Doc how to tail a winch, we had Al to the block and safely back on deck in no time.

    With the foresail done the main should go easy. Revving the new halyard through and splicing it to the gaff, I started to overhaul the old halyard. Now the new line seemed to be going through a block used for the peak system. Just not possible! Hauling back on new line the old followed. Wait a minute; I'm working with the throat halyard, not the peak. Wrong! Somehow the lines were passing through the middle block for the peak. Checking and rechecking to figure out what the hex went wrong. Then the light of knowledge lit up! Stupid! When mating the two halyards I inadvertently mated the new line to the peak halyard instead of the throat. This started when I took the halyard from the belaying pin, not checking that I had the right one. You always secure the throat halyard forward of the peak on the pin rail, like the way they are on the gaff boom. The next cardinal rule is you always look aloft and check if they are fouled. The only way to right the wrong is to cut the splice and start over. That would use up a lot of line which I might not have. Here again off to Al, head down feeling lower than whale shit which is on the bottom of the ocean. The next fix is to go back aloft to retrieve it and pass it through the right block. Looking aloft Al said that the halyard above was strong enough for him to use. I in turn did not feel it was large enough in diameter to handle or strong enough. But Al held his ground, and once more he was to be hauled up. I had no sooner started than a stranger jumped aboard taking the tail of the halyard. As soon as he leaned over to take the line I could smell the alcohol on his breath, straight whiskey. Should I tell him no thanks? Or work with him and be sure I had full control of the halyard; I only had to keep tension on the winch to keep Al safe. Thank God Al yelled down he had everything straightened out and could come down. Once on deck we thanked the gentleman and found out that he lived on a sailboat here in the yard. He and his wife were the ones that had stopped the day before asking about the boat. Finished at last! Not that it was a big or hard job, cleaning everything up and stowing away the old halyard for some future time. Nothing on a boat is thrown away; old cordage can be made into mattes, chafing gear, quick fix lashings, or as said, give a man enough rope and he will hang himself. Long after being home Liz and I drove out to Plattsmouth, Nebraska for her mother's ninetieth birthday. She had informed everyone that she wished to go canoeing, so off we went with a kayak lashed to the roof of Liz's Element, using part of the old halyard to secure it. Well, traveling at sixty or so was just too much for the old halyard, it parted, luckily just one part with no real danger of losing the kayak, a lot better than a gaff boom letting go.

 This was one day I was sure glad was over, I sure had sweated, not because of work but because of the work I had created. First a much-needed shower, then a stiff drink. At the Tree House Mark was first to ask if we had finished our work. Evidently he had told the gang of his visit and seemed impressed with the use of the running rigging as a device to go aloft and the amount of splicing and whipping needed. Evidently he had never been on a boat when line work or the use of running rigging was being done during maintenance. Next to him on the bar was a fat paperback book titled *The Unlikely Voyage of Jack De Crow* that he was reading and thought we would like. Sure enough it was our type of reading; it's about A. J. Mackinnon, who sailed a Mirror dink from North Wales to the Black Sea, a good find for fine reading for those of us who like nothing better than messing about with boats. This evening we were not going to congregate for lengthy gams, only a drink, dinner, and a few laughs. We told them that we would be sailing in the early morning, before daybreak so we could be at Hell Gate at slack water. Smiling, the old man agreed. All too fast four bells - 10:00 bar time - was sounding announcing our time of departure; farewells, handshakes, and we were off.

WAYPOINT 16
L 40° 50' 29" N λ 73° 46' 54" W

At four in the morning 'our is begun
To the cockpit the waisters for buckets must run,
Our fore and main topmen so loudly do bawl,
For sand and for holystones, both large an' small.
> "The Fancy Frigate," *The Bosun's Locker*, Stan Hugill

Our destination is Cape May, New Jersey with no stops planned. If everything goes right and our departure time is correct, we should have a favorable tide all the way to Sandy Hook. From City Island to Hell Gate on the East River is 11 miles, to the Hudson River 18 miles down the East River. The ebb on the Hudson River can flow at 1.4 knots in our favor; at the Hell Gate on East River, the mean velocity strength of current during ebb can reach 4.5 knots. I have never seen this amount of current at Hell Gate due to the fact we have always planned our transit at slack. When reading *The Cruising Guide to the New England Coast* you come across some interesting facts. The Hudson River is one of the deepest canyons in the world reaching a depth of 3600 feet, a thousand feet deeper than the Royal Gorge in Colorado. Oh well, we hadn't figured to anchor anyway. In the book *The Rudder Treasury* Thomas Fleming Day talks about how Long Island Sound was once called The Devil's Belt. An area from Hell Gate to the eastern end of Long Island, if you think of it, the ocean is at each end and surrounds Long Island like a belt. No one knows for sure where the name comes from but old Sea Cards, early books, and charts refer to the Sound in this way. Down through the years many a mariner used word of mouth and very little recorded information to navigate through these tricky currents and shoals.

From the Free Enterprise Forever! "Scientific American" in the 19th Century lets you go back in time. The great obstruction impeding ship movement from the East River to Long Island Sound was a promontory of Long Island called Hallett's Point; it reaches out into East River towards Ward's Island, which occupies three fifths of the width of the river along with some large continually dangerous rocks. So in 1848 the United States Navy presented a document giving a description of the course and strength of the tidal current and dangers to navigation. Disturbance caused by the rocks such as Pot Rock and Frying Pan which were pointed shaped, creating whirlpools and radical change in direction of current flow affecting a vessel's track and control along with Way's Reef characterized more like a ledge. Their recommendations were to blast out the rock and open up the main channel. A submarine blasting to scatter the rock and the cavity to revive it would sufficiently clear the channel to a depth for common vessels. Also it would increase facilities for naval defense. We had homeland security back then, too; nothing changes. On August 1869 at Halletts Point, a coffer dam was built of heavy timbers and bolted to the river bottom. Then the river was pumped out so miners could start to cut through the quartz rock to make a cavity within the formation of rock overhead. Then 23 charges made up of 10 ounces of Rendrock or Vulcan powder (nitro-glycerin compounds) were set off in a simultaneous explosion dropping the mountain of rock into the cavity they had dug. Here we are traversing the same waters; it not only has a different name but what a difference in navigation. Well, one more interesting leg of this trip under my belt.

There's something about rising before daylight, this is the time to come home, not to go out. Al and I were up before three bells, 05:30 ship's time, coffee on the wait, first things first. Being bow in, we first had to turn ship and face out. They had rafted a motor yacht to another one made fast to the opposite pier. Looking over the situation, we warped her around the piling on our starboard quarter. This took a little doing as our spar length and the space between the moored boats were about the same. One nice thing, even though it was before sun up, visibility was bright and clear. As we motored out, clearing the breakwater barge and steering for the Stepping Stones, Al was setting the reefed main, getting us in motoring mode.

Our first encounter with commercial traffic was staring me in the face. About two miles ahead I could see his red and green, on the barge and side lights on the tug, plus his two vertical white lights. A maritime Christmas tree. We were face to face, and it was my call. Figuring he would swing to starboard to enter Long Island Sound, I swung to starboard so we would pass red to red properly. Sure enough we cleared with plenty of room and I felt he had no trouble with our action. I like an early encounter; it gets you in the right mindset, pay attention! At the same time Al had gone below making coffee, checking position, and then handing me out a coffee for a mug up. Getting brighter and more traffic as we worked between Throgs Neck and Little Neck Bay into the East River was the beginning of the real river traffic. Already the shoreline was changing more to commercial. From here we would leave Rikers Island to port, lot more traffic but no planes from La Guardia. At times Al pointed out the landmarks such as the North and South Brother Islands as we passed between them on to the Middle Ground.

Our next major spot is passing through the Hell Gate. I always check the tail on the marks as we pass to keep aware of current and direction. Nearing the Hell Gate we were carrying some current but only what Al had predicted. Areas like this are hard to explain, the smells, the buildings, old, new, falling down, being built, trash barges being filled. Buoys of all kinds leading to everywhere, placed on rock piles, towers, on shore; some I had no idea what they meant. Sure glad Al had been here recently and had time to check the chart and plotter. Sliding down the river like Mark Twain, not a care in the world, just a different world and time. No mud banks, sand bars, or floating trees, yet quite a different type of obstacles at hand, all kinds of commercial traffic in all directions, then throw in good weather which has brought out all sizes of pleasure craft and all in a hurry. A lot of my friends have been stopped and made to wait or change direction by the Coast Guard since 9/11. What a break! No hassle, no detouring, just running free. Passing between Roosevelt Island and Manhattan Island brought back memories of my first trip through here. We had a crewmember on board who lived in Manhattan, and as we motorsailed along he would name the streets, point out the different buildings, and give us tidbits of information.

Passing under the Williamsburg, Manhattan, and finally the Brooklyn Bridge put us at the South Street Museum, where the schooners *Lettie G. Howard* and *Pioneer* are berthed. Next pier upstream is the *Clipper City* out of Baltimore. *Pioneer* and the *Lettie* have both been to Baltimore for the Great Chesapeake Bay Schooner Race. Arriving early in Baltimore the *Pioneer* volunteered to work in our school education program. I have crewed twice on the *Lettie* for the race, and then I helped to deliver her back to be down-rigged for the winter. *Clipper City*, once a Baltimore based schooner, has also done the race, yet I have never sailed her, only partied on her at fundraisers.

Sliding past Diamond Reef between the Battery and Governors Island is the last of the East River. But this can be one busy place with all the ferries, tugs, and in and out commercial shipping. I wonder why they call the shoal Diamond Reef, maybe because of all the diamond engagement rings thrown off the ferries. After leaving all this astern, we still have to pass through a fairly heavily used anchorage. Some of the anchored vessels we had to bring close aboard as we worked our way through the area, always checking that no one pops out from behind the boat we are coming around. If we had had time to look up each foreign flag on the ships it would have been an interesting trip around the world, this is truly the gateway to the world.

We have had a good push from the current but still no lift from the wind, on the other hand no wind shear off the buildings or wind generated seas. Now in a more open area with shorelines farther apart and the sun at almost noon, I was hoping for more air. Oh well, the little Yammy is purring right along, what a good crewmember. The run from here to the Verrazano Narrows Bridge is a straight run and very little traffic. Al set the fore to see if it will give us a little lift, maybe a little but it does feel better under more sail.

Clearing the bridge the Narrows opens much wider, and the further towards Sandy Hook the more the waves will be affected by the ocean surge. The first time I sailed in this area was in the 'sixties on the schooner *Variant*. Coming in after dark, I had to find the Marine Basin boat yard. Knowing Coney Island was astern off our starboard, we ran parallel to the shoreline looking for an American flag on a white flag pole lit up. This belonged to the Excelsior Yacht Club, which was right next door to the Marine Basin. Sure enough, up came the light and next to it a high wooden sea wall. We were told to make fast to the wall just in front of a sunken tug with a red light on it. Ok, wall but no red light! Working close to the wall I swung over to the wall using a halyard, luckily the top of the wall was wide enough to drive a truck out on. Sure enough inside the basin was the red light, no tug, I guess it's completely underwater. All we had to do is motor up along the wall until we could turn into the basin. What you won't do when young and dumb.

WAYPOINT 17
L 40° 34' 45" N λ 74° 01' 55" W

And now look aloft, me boys, every one,
All hands to make sail, going large is the song;
From under two reefs in our tops'ls we lie,
Like a cloud all our canvas in a moment must fly
> "The Fancy Frigate," *The Bosun's Locker*, Stan Hugill

From here to Sandy Hook through the Lower Bay was a piece of cake, no change of course for traffic, weather holding, and right on our predicted time. Now everyone has heard all kinds of tales about Sandy Hook, this is the place it will happen if it is in your stack of cards. For me the passages around the Hook have been pleasant, but once it did get a little hairy. I was on the schooner *Rose-Mary-Roth* with Richard Hudson working our way south against a southerly. When we cleared Sandy Hook it was good sailing; we knew the weather was to change but felt we would be ahead of it. Being well east and south of Sandy Hook I went below for some shut-eye. Returning on deck I realized Richard had put a reef in the main and fore and was still holding on to the forestays'l, and we were still rail down. Asking why he hadn't called me to help to reef, no big deal, I single hand all the time. Giving me the latest update on position and weather, then asking to be called if the wind or seas built he went below. Watching astern at the weather I could see lots of lightning lighting up the storm clouds, but no rain and maybe a little more wind. After awhile Richard came back on deck asking if everything was ok, or did we need another reef. I don't think so, I've been looking astern and the storm seems to be going north along the shoreline. Wrong! With that we were smothered in rain and wind, lee deck awash, sheets slacked, letting her have her head to stand her up so sails could be dropped, it all happened in a flash. It only lasted a short time and we were back under shortened sail. Wind before rain, storm short lived. The next morning, still reefed and running in dusty weather and bruising a few confused seas, Richard was on his Blackberry checking the weather and distance to Atlantic City. At the same time we were discussing Tristan Jones's books and his adventures. Most people feel he is full of bullshit, but if he is why hasn't someone come forward, after all he is only writing about things and places in our time. Some one has! I just sent an e-mail to Denise to order the book so it will be there when I get home. What a world we live in, reaching out to the world with the touch of a finger but living in the environment of old salts of yesterday.

Rounding the Hook, setting a new course to run down the Jersey coast the plotter laid us on the return course of the one coming north; in fact, we've been on it since entering the East River. This motor sailing lays a straight course line so the kids watching the spotter know when we are motoring. We did get the last laugh when sailing north along the coast, wing and wing or broad reaching straight as an arrow. For now seas smooth, wind light, accompanying vessels seem to be heading south like us, maybe they too are heading for Cape May. Idle time makes idle minds, remembering back to the trip north when we had rendezvoused with the schooner *Winfield Lash*, she on her return trip from the Bahamas. I had referred to her earlier when going north and said I would come back to her. Well, things are at ease motoring along in a big open sea, so here is the tale.

The image of the schooner *Bluenose* on the Canadian dime was the ember in Dave Clarke's heart fanned into flame by William Atkins' 1927 design of the schooner *Chantey*, later the fire of desire was fueled by the agreement with Mr. Winfield Lash of Lash Brothers to build a modified version. Winnie, as Mr. Lash went by, would build hull, deck, and cabin trunk. Never shying away from work, Dave was to find and deliver the agreed types of wood such as white oak, black locust, and anything else along with working alongside Winnie. Off he went picking through lumberyards, antique shops, and derelict boats such as the 81' steam yacht *Sayonara*. Buying salvage rights to the *Sayonara* and agreeing to have the whole boat go away ate up a lot more time than estimated. But here again disassembling was a real learning experience; here were valuable techniques that he could incorporate. Yielding a now-rare Andaman padauk wood that finished to a rich vermillion color would add to the unique interior. His quest to find exceptional wood and unusual pieces of interior and deck hardware took him from Florida to London, finding elaborately carved walnut panels, a Chinese table that would be disassembled and a Baby Blake marine head all to enhance her interior. Always keeping surrounded by people with the knowledge and skills he needed such as John Atkin, Olin Stephens, Paul Rollins, and Bud McIntosh filled all the voids of his knowledge on boat building. The project always on his mind, he would go to wooden boat shows, museums, any place to gain information and confidence. Having an artistic eye and craftsman's hands he made all the patterns for the elaborate bronze castings for belaying pins, Turk's head knobs for the skylight, and the Mermaid binnacle base. All of this work and dedication created a piece of serviceable art that was featured in *WoodenBoat* magazine (number 166 May/June 2002.) Being satisfied in accomplishing the construction stage, he was off sailing her throughout New England, then to Nova Scotia, and is now returning from the Bahamas.

The schooner *Chantey* David talked about I had helped deliver down the Hudson River to Baltimore. In David's searching he met the daughter of Henry M. Plummer, Jr. Henry's father and he had sailed a 24 ft. 6 in. 30 year old, old-fashioned Cape Cod catboat named *Mascot* from New Bedford, Massachusetts to Miami, Florida during the year

1912-1913. I think it was Alice H. Plummer who gave the book, a ditty bag, and the box compass from the *Mascot* to David. This is one of the first books I had read and I still have it. I enjoyed it so much I always suggest it to other sailors who seek adventure with a challenge. David handed me the compass, yes, the very compass off *Mascot*. In the issue of *WoodenBoat* that featured the *Winfield Lash,* the last page Save-A- Classic was advertising for a prospective restorer for the 61 ft. racing sloop *Highland Light*. In 1939, Dudley Wolfe bequeathed her to the U.S. Naval Academy in Annapolis. After regattas, the Academy held cocktail parties on her. I remember walking her decks and the good times. Life is strange and truth is stranger then fiction.

Preparing for nightfall, which was not far off, Al went below as I had the first watch. Sitting on my perch, the *Dragon* under command of the autopilot glided right along. Scanning the horizon to get a position on the accompanying vessels or any northbound traffic I hadn't seen was a pleasant way to enjoy the evening. When running at night we have the radar on and about every hour we scan out a couple of miles to check for incoming mail. If a target shows up and appears to be converging on our course, we monitor it till it has passed or moved out of our danger zone. The new radios have this AIS built in: interfaced to the plotter it will show an icon of a vessel, and putting the cursor on the icon will give you the vessel's name, type, speed, and direction. It also predetermines the point of collision. This is a great advantage, when at the wheel all you have to do is scan out four or five miles and see if there's any traffic, if so check it out or leave the plotter at this scale and you know exactly where the other vessel is. Only an aid, look, check, and beware, of course; the surface of the ocean washes away all mistakes. The fun part of this is because we do not have a sender, if we change course the computer for the system does not know and still computes us showing the collision as a ship-shaped icon in red with an X over it. The *Green Dragon* puts all her faith in the man at the wheel to guide her safely through his watch while the rest of the crew is below, stay awake.

All of the vessels in company have sail on but are too far off to see if they are motor sailing as we are or if there is enough wind to sustain speed. Off our starboard quarter a catamaran was working off shore and making time, surely will be abeam then ahead before long, here again she can out-sail us. We very close hauled her on a close reach, her best point of sail, and again she could have her motor purring. As evening twilight faded, the other vessels' running lights appeared and surrounded the night horizon. Depth perception at night can be misleading so as darkness comes on, I try to keep scanning the horizon or shoreline till my eyes adjust. The ones astern and to starboard seemed the same distance off and the ones to port might be working ahead. The *Dragon* is a very comfortable boat whether under sail or power, nice response from the wheel, her roll, and her forgivingness when under a press of sail is pleasant. All of this you have to take into consideration when everything is at peace - stay awake, pay attention, and keep your mind on the job. At times like this I think of sea chanties or make up new verses.

No Grave

No grave is going to keep me down
Ain't no grave going to keep me down

I don't want to just lay around,
I want to be here when the rum is served around

A rogue sailor wants to be on the open sea not hard aground
Lay me not in a six by three, in the deep and dark ground

Put me on a schooner fit and sound
Driving hard full and by, rail down Oh what a sound

There's more women and fun to be found
No searching for life, mine's been found

Wine, women, and song till the sun goes down
Oh for the love of a woman when she takes you down

To sail in a full blown gale and run like the fox and hound
No papers or pedigree just an old sea dog, just a hound

Give me the open sea not anchored down in some port or town
Just one more chance to drive hard a schooner that's sound.

Jay Irwin

Well it ain't much, but it kept me awake when needed.

WAYPOINT 18
L 40° 06' 56" N λ 73° 52' 14" W

The moving moon went up the sky,
And nowhere did abide:
Softly she was going up,
And a star or two beside –
> *Rime of the Ancient Mariner*, Samuel T. Coleridge

    This is a milk run for the *Dragon*, if one looked at her log they could wrongly think of her as a coastal trader. Steering steadily south down the silver path of the new half moon which is now directly over Cape May, our point of destination is all I need, no GPS, plotter, just an old boat and old ways. The half moon was bright and a nice reflection on the water yet the horizon was black, no distinction between water and sky, so others' running lights stood out quite bright. Wind, what there is, the same; sea conditions the same, clear with bright stars to navigate by. Log entry if we kept one, Al and I just inform each other when changing watches. We point out the location of vessels around us, show the hits on the radar or plotter, and confirm position.

    This part of the run down the coast is not that interesting at night, the shoreline has no towns or anything of size lit up until we reach Atlantic City. Our main concern is fishing vessels: when working they're all lit up, when under way only navigation lights. Another real concern is unlit marks, but that is on any body of water. Every now and then you will bring a fishermen's net or trap marker close aboard. Once one came down the starboard side flag waving and close aboard! Startled I took it for someone alongside waving, what a wake up call. Everything staying the same I should be on deck until just north of Atlantic City. We have been blessed with good weather, no rain, warm, and clear. Some nights you're bundled up in layers of clothes, foul weather gear along with your harness making movement confined. Another standing rule, call below if sail change or forward deck work has to be performed. Al at times would stick his head out of the companionway, slipping me a cookie, asking if everything's all right, a quiet check for our position on the plotter, then back to his bunk. We don't stick to a standard watch system of four on four off, just retired loose-footed vagabonds' rules. When you are the only one on deck it's quite a pleasure, but you have full responsibility for life, limb, boat, and more so at night. Mother Nature dictates the rules of the sea and who are we not to obey rules.

Some boats overtaking, others seem to be falling back, air up a little more, not enough to wake Al to see if we could put old Yammy to sleep. If we sail we probably will have to fall off, then work back to make Cape May entrance. I don't think the boats overtaking us are sailing only; their heading seems to be the same. Returning to the cockpit candy and a cookie in hand, Al asking if I wanted anything more. After a full update, bilge check, engine check, and agreeing there's not enough air to fool with, he took the wheel. Ok, I got her, you hit the bunk. When underway at night I usually take the port settee berth, stay dressed or in foul weather gear, only removing coat and boots. That way I can be up on deck in a flash if needed. But this night was so pleasant all I had to do was kick off my shoes, hit the bunk, pull the opened sleeping bag up over me, and in two seconds I was out in never never land or wherever we go when sleeping. Waking and returning to the cockpit I asked Al if that wasn't Wildwood or Wildwood Crest off our starboard quarter, sure enough I was just about to call you.

Looking ahead, we both were looking for a red flasher "2cm" FL 2.5s just outside the Cape May Inlet. We really don't have to honor this mark, but if you work up close and have it abeam you will see the range lights leading you into the Inlet off the opposite beam. The moon was now southwest of the Inlet and just about to set below the horizon, giving us no silver path to follow and making it quite dark, really the black of night. As we turned to starboard and looked into the Inlet, we were right in the middle and on the range. Knowing the breakwater is a favorite fishing spot and as we were right at the time for a tide change, I was looking for small sport fishing boats. Sure enough, one was fishing along the south side of the jetty working along to the outside end of the jetty. As he worked around the end of the jetty, I realized he wasn't showing any running lights or they sure weren't bright. I asked Al if he saw him, commenting we were the privileged vessel right now but if he turned to go in we would become the overtaking vessel, making us the burdened vessel. All of this in close quarters in pitch black of night and possibly a tricky current. When entering the Inlet you have the markers FL R 4s 30ft "4" 6m and FL G 4s 37ft 7m "5" Horn on the ends of the jetty. Then farther inside is an unlighted red number RN "2", then just past it to port is G "3", which is also unlighted. Just ahead is the bright red flashing lower range light FL (2+1) R 6s "C" PA about eye level that seems to be closer than it really is. This is when you swing to port and look down the channel into the harbor. Then you line up the lighted channel marks "4pa" and "5pa". Next you look for the unlighted marks, three in all to starboard, then a green to port. The only lighted one ahead is number "10", which you must honor, then turn to starboard hard, and you enter the Cape May Canal. We entered the Inlet trying to read the water at the entrance to see if the whirlpool or disturbance of water from the current trying to ebb against the ocean was going to set us on the north or south side of the Inlet. But at the same time we were paying more attention to the fishing boat; we were kind of coming in by the seat of our pants. When you stare at something, as you move along you will unintentionally steer for it. If closing in on, we'll say the windward mark, along with other boats about to converge at the same time, you should not keep looking at the mark; you look out past the mark or you will definitely be too close to pass between it and the other boats. Without realizing it, we were both watching the fishermen instead of only one and the other one steering and looking ahead. It only takes a minute and you can go from ok to oh shit. We both realized at the same time, as the fishermen hailed us to head off as we were heading into the jetty. Turning to starboard to regain the middle of the channel and paying attention to the range and plotter, we focused on finding the red unlighted buoy. Finding it, we then saw the green and turned to run down the channel.

WAYPOINT 19
L 38° 57' 02" N λ 74° 52' 32" W

Water, water everywhere,
All the boards did shrink;
Water, water everywhere,
Nor any drop to drink.
> *Rime of the Ancient Mariner*, Samuel T. Coleridge

Believe me, once inside the harbor this is a persnickety piece of thin-spread moisture. There just is no depth to the water out of the channel. For a home port for heavy commercial fishing vessels and a well-used route by transit vessels, they sure keep the bottom close to the surface.

As we turned at the green "3pa", we just could not see the unlighted reds or the anchorage to port of the area of the red buoyed section. Nothing was silhouetted against the background, either black space or the lighted marinas to the west or the Coast Guard Station to the east. The moon was ahead of us and just about to set. I told Al to steer for the moon, for it seemed to be in mid-channel for us, and I would scan for the marks. You just could not see the anchorage, far less see if anyone was anchored. Making things worse, the Coast Guard station is further down the channel and lit up with super bright lights that blind you when trying to see along the shore, mainly the anchorage. About halfway into the channel, the moon set. Looking to starboard for the damned day markers, we worked too close to the edge of the channel and took the middle mark close aboard, making a quick correction to get back in deep water, saving grounding. As I said, we could see the marinas to starboard and in between them the red light showing the center of the bridge crossing over the Cape May Canal. But right in our immediate area we just could not identify the limits of the channel. We had cut our speed down to about three knots when entering the Inlet and were running a lot slower now that we were in the harbor; at times we were almost stopped, feeling our way down the channel.

Our first intentions were to stay underway clear through to the Delaware Bay, catching the flood tide that would carry us to the C&D canal and then into the Elk River, which is the head of the Chesapeake Bay. Our timing was right on, for the flood would start at about two thirty a.m.. Now with the confusion and unsureness, we felt it better to come about, locate the anchorage, get some sleep, and regroup. Motoring 180 degrees from our original course (a first on this trip) with the Coast Guard Station to starboard, we could just make out the images of the anchored boats. Our next concern was not to anchor too close to the channel because the larger fishing boats come through the harbor with their outriggers down for stability, which means they might just wipe us out. Last year Al said he had been rudely awakened by one such fishing vessel's horn; evidently he felt insecure passing the anchorage. Once in the anchorage area, trying to judge swinging room between the other vessels but not grounding was a real challenge. Depth perception was just hard to judge. As clear as it was, the darkness just obscured all the reflected light. Finally the hook was down and *Dragon*, with the help of the current, was hauling back on her rode in a secure spot. I hope. Looking around, checking twice, making sure everything was nice, now it was time to get some shuteye for the night.

I don't think Al got much shuteye, for he heard the outbound fishing vessels passing and said at one time we had swung a lot closer to our neighbor than he liked. Next on the agenda was a mug up, then we hashed over everything that had happened last night. First, both of us paid too much attention to the fishing boat and then we realized neither one of us remembers seeing the starboard jetty entrance light; it must have been out. From our experience in the fog we both felt it was not easy steering with the plotter; the delay in the signal for the heading makes for far too much over-correction. It showed exactly where we were, but the cursor's position in relation to the actual position of the boat in such close quarters cannot be relied on; we feel you must have visual identification. Maybe we relied too much on experience and in reality should have studied the chart more and approached the Inlet as though it were our first time in. The darkness we had no control over, but it sure took us by surprise. The sky and horizon were crystal clear, yet the immediate area, as I said, was black as ink. Have you ever gotten up at night and started for the bathroom knowing you were in the bedroom but couldn't find your way, just couldn't find the furniture leading you to the door, just lost and confused, then finding something you could identify with? The one thing good about all of this, we worked together, telling each other what we saw and asking each other if he saw it the way you did. Only once I had told Al to steer to starboard, the bow started to swing to port, and then I said no, go the other way. This was a confusing reply, and I should have stuck to starboard. Little things like this can lead to sudden misfortune. The one thing we both knew is that it is one shallow area to pass through. From the channel to the Corinthian Yacht Club you have to pick your way through the shoal spots, some two feet and less, just to get into one of the marinas, especially Utsch's Marina on port side. When entering the Cape May Channel you have to start into the channel, then turn to port, then follow the breakwater to the opening, all of this with no marks skirting a foot and a half depth in this area.

Al had already been on the computer checking the times of the next flood. The midday one was too early in the day for us to make comfortably, but he had another concern. He had been paying close attention to the amount of water we were taking since leaving New York. Now the *Dragon* has a very unique bilge pump system. For major pumping there is an inch and a quarter discharge pump running from amidships aft and out the exhaust, but when the pump shuts off the water in the hose flows back into the bilge, making for unnecessary short time running. To correct this, Al installed a three-quarter inch pump in the galley area that discharges into the galley drain and has no feedback; he calls it a sipping pump. This is in the deeper part of the bilge, so if kept dry the big pump is not needed. The next thing that is nice is when you move about in the galley area and change the boat's trim, the pump is activated and you hear the water flowing through the galley drain, giving you a heads up on the amount of water being removed. All wooden boats, especially old wooden boats, make water while underway. The twisting of the hull, the movement of inside ballast lying on the planking, caulking worked loose or pulled loose by fish feeding on it, worse yet old fastenings, all lead to leakage. Al had heard the sipping pump coming on all night and was timing it since being up. So now was the time to try and find the culprit. I went forward and took up the floor boards forward of the mast to see if leakage was this far forward. Oh yeah, sure enough water could be seen flowing between the ballast, working its way aft, not a lot, but we were at anchor with no way on. With the accumulation of water in the lower section of the bilge you would not see movement of water, indicating leakage in this area. The main pump was turned on to clear the water out of this section of bilge, but no leakage could be seen. Around the mast steps there was no sign of a leak, but aft in the lazarette a small amount of water was working its way to the bilge. We had worked the boat on the way here, but definitely not hard.

    For sure this was going to be a lay day. Checking for a marina, Al found the phone number for Roseman's Boat Yard and explained our situation, and by any chance could they haul us if needed. They informed him there wasn't enough water in Spicer Creek Canal for us to reach their yard as the tide had been lower then normal in the last couple of days, and he didn't know of anyone that could haul us. Here is where the heavy burden of responsibility falls on the shoulder of the owner, skipper, of the vessel. First, we are about half way between Manchester, Massachusetts and Norfolk, Virginia, with a race to do from Baltimore to Portsmouth, Virginia. Second, the race is not that important, but the distance to Norfolk is the same. If the *Dragon* does need work, should we turn tail and make the run back to Crocker's in Manchester, go to Baltimore, or try to go the distance? The real solution is to determine what is going on and where or who to fix it. Setting here at anchor, she just isn't taking in that much water. When faced with this type of problem everything has to be considered, the if, how, and buts, of what really is happening, how will weather and sea conditions affect our stability and integrity of hull and rigging? Will steady running tighten a sprung seam or work a sprung plank, has a fastening let go, is a keel bolt about to let go. After fifty years of slopping around in boats and almost that much time working in boat yards, you would think I could find the culprit. Surely the rabbit in the stem at the cutwater is a potential, the garboard strake seams along the keel, the horn timber, and the counter seams are always working loose. For sure she doesn't have nail rot, not the way they check her at Crocker's. But nowhere is there enough running water to follow to the leak.

    I've been on a lot of leaking boats, I mean real leakers that leaked when you left and leaked when you arrived and leaked while there. They kind of filtered the water, maybe a cross of an oyster and a boat, each did the same but different, one sat still on the bottom to do its work, the other doing the same traveling across the surface taking in water on one side, filtering it, and pumping it out the other. When you sail on a potential crab crusher you kind of learn to live with it, it seems to be her personality and life goes on. But when a boat is kept in Bristol fashion and in tip-top shape as the *Dragon* and her ways change, you pay attention. Yet again, she just wasn't shipping that much water. As Gordon Lightfoot said in his song *Christian Island*,

> She's a good old boat and she'll stay afloat
> Through the toughest gales and keep smilin'
> But for one more day she would like to stay
> In the lee of Christian Island [Cape May]

Al has a lot on his mind and doesn't need outside input; at a time like this, the crew needs to be like children, seen but not heard. I started looking around to find some little job or project that had been put aside to do at a later date; now was the time. Working on deck, whipping bitter ends of miscellaneous lines to get rid of unsightly cow tails, putting Turk's heads on the foresails sheet pony traveler to act as shock absorbers, and checking that the anchor was still secured properly. All the while the old *Dragon* just lay at anchor hardly taking any water at all, just waiting for our next move. Al in the meantime was at the computer checking the times of flood on the Delaware Bay to calculate our time of departure and how close we would be to the ebb at the Chesapeake and Delaware Canal. In the past Al always stayed on the north side of the Delaware so he could go into some of the rivers to do some gunkholing. I, in turn, had always gone straight through to at least Middle River, which was our intent for the upcoming leg. On a six knot boat, if you leave the western end of the Cape May Canal during the last hour of ebb of the Delaware, this gives you time to work out to the main channel and the ebbing current is too weak and getting weaker as you make your way to the channel. When you work into the main channel, the flood will have started building, carrying you right along. At each elbow along the channel, the current becomes hydraulic because of the amount of water being rammed through the narrow sections of the elbows, giving more speed to the current. If you hit it right with no head winds, you will arrive at the C & D Canal at the beginning of the ebb, which will carry you west to the headwater of the Chesapeake Bay at time of ebb. During the whole trip you have a favorable current and really make time. Because Al had never gone straight through, he couldn't comprehend how much faster it is with the favoring current. When checking the current tables for six knots along the distance from canal to canal, they don't take into consideration the extra time made up because of the favorable current so it looks like you miss the change of current at the C&D. Last night the flood was around two or three a.m. or about, so it will be about an hour later tomorrow night.

 Both of us were sitting in the cockpit discussing the pro and cons of leaving in the early morning and if we could make the whole trip on one change of current, but everything had to go just right. If we did get a favorable wind we would probably gain more speed and use less, if any, fuel and possibly be early at the C&D. We both noticed at the same time a Johnboat with two men and a dog coming toward us and preparing to come alongside. Taking their line and placing a fender over the side, they told us that they were from Roseman's boat yard and came out to check on the boat and our welfare. Seeing that we had everything under control and not in any immediate danger, they started asking about the boat. First they were concerned about the leaking and what we thought was the trouble, then they asked when, where, and by whom she was built. It is always the same when people find out how long Al has owned the *Dragon* and how much she is used and the distances traveled. People sure look up to a captain and his boat when they know that they are not armchair sailors but doers. We in turn were asking them about Cape May and the type of boats they mainly work on and how involved they get in rebuilding or repairing. It seemed they do just about everything, as it is a full service yard. I asked them if by any chance they had any shavings or sawdust from the thickness planer handy so we could dust the hull. Laughing, they said. 'Oh, you know that old trick!' and sure, they had plenty and would be glad to bring a couple of bags out to us. Right away Al asked what I intended to do. Back home the old timers had taught me to take a pan on a long handle full of shavings and slide it under the boat holding it against the hull, then shake it as I pulled it down and out from under the boat. The shavings float up against the hull and are sucked into the leaking seams, then swell and chock up the leak. This really works if the boat is lying at rest, but if underway there's a good chance that it will be washed out. Back in the days of sail many a schooner was laid up on a mud flat and allowed to settle with the tide so the mud could be forced into the seams, a poor man's caulking. If dusted before hauling a planked hull, the sawdust or shavings will be in the seams that need tending. We offered to come and get the shavings, but they said they could be over and back before we could get the inflatable overboard and that they would be back after lunch.

If everything stays the same and we are successful in stopping or slowing the leak, it looks like a go. Our next obstacle is the three-mile Cape May Canal; it is narrow and shallow, just a bitch of a ditch. High sides and no lights other then navigation lights at the bridges and carrying a depth of nine feet dropping to eight with an old railroad swing bridge having a Hor Cl of fifty feet and only a four foot Vert Cl. Our departure will be at the same time as last night when we were feeling our way around and possibly will be just as dark. Watching the surrounding anchored boats preparing to leave and then heading for the Delaware, we were wondering why they would fight the current as there was no air here and the weather report reported nothing on the Bay. I guess some people just don't like night running, especially with the possibility of heavy traffic north and south bound if you stay in the channel. Also, what is left of the major lighthouses is interesting and worth seeing during a day run. If they stay closer to the north shore and in shallower water, they'll miss a lot of the strong current. Oh well, when lying around with no task at hand, it's nice to check out the other man's boat, ponder about his reasons and ways of doing things. Many times I have picked up a new trick or system. For me, I think I'll have a snack, hit the bunk, get some shuteye, and be bright-eyed and bushy-tailed for the night run. After a good nap, out in the cockpit with Al I got caught up on what had happened. First the crew from Roseman's came back with five or six bags of shavings and two cold beers; second, a twenty-foot or so cat boat from the private anchorage further down the channel worked her way up to the *Dragon* for a look-see. She was a gaff rigged, traditional center boarder, being single-handed quite well. Al said as she tacked around checking us out she was picture perfect, well trimmed, and slid along on a nice heel working through the anchorage putting on a nice show of seamanship. Although she never rounded up or hove-to to within speaking distance, just a smile and wave was enough for each skipper to compliment the other. It's times and places like this that you really get the full enjoyment out of the boat and trip. Business at hand, we turned to just how we were going to go about dusting down the hull. We seemed to be at slack tide so most of the shavings should not be carried downstream on the current away from the hull. If we put a tear in the bag of shavings and tied the bag to the boat hook, we could probably reach far enough under the hull from the cockpit and foredeck. Dusting mostly in the stern on both sides, then some in the bow, we felt we had done fairly well and still had some sawdust saved for a later date if needed. Some stew, bread, and coffee, then early to bed and early to rise: we have a favorable current to catch before sunrise.

 Hearing Al in the galley I knew it was time to roll my sleeping bag up, have a mug up, and ready the anchor to come up. Al had already been out on the Internet and it looked like it was going to be a fine day. Light and variable winds from East to South South east, flat mild seas, clear skies. But oh was it dark, the same as last night, only this time we were mentally and physically ready to take on the canal section. Al said that the sipping pump had hardly come on last night and felt that the sawdust and shavings had done the trick. We both agreed that the water we saw coming from the bow area was water trapped there while we were rolling around underway and it had to drain from between the frames and ballast. The ol' Yammy purring away, the anchor choked up and ready to be broken loose, seeing the channel marker FL R 2.5s "10" PA farther ahead of us, we were ready. Al signaled to break her loose, and as the Coast Guard would say, we were now legally underway. Once in the Cape May Canal visibility was poor at best; it was hard to distinguish the water's edge and the canal's banks, and keeping in the center was tricky because you had no horizon ahead of you. Shortly we could see the lights for the swing bridge and sure enough, the starboard side of the opening was out. The bridge is kept open unless a train is to use it; the section that swings is in the middle of the channel making east and west bound lanes. But at night the pilings and structure blend right in with the background, and the lights flashing at eye level make strange shadows and as you get closer they tend to blind you. When you're entering the opening, that fifty foot horizontal clearance does not look that wide and you get the feeling that you are moving faster than you are, a real relief once through. Our next puzzle was a red flashing light on our starboard side just before the Cape May-Lewes Ferry Terminal. It sure looked too close to the shoreline for us to honor it and no sign of it on the plotter or chart. As we bore down on it, we could see storage tanks further back on shore and decking coming from the shore out to the light. (Since being back from the trip I have talked to a lot people who have been through the canal and all feel the same way - why is it red, it could be green, amber, even white.) From here the ferry terminal really stands out and lights up the full width of the cannel. Further on you see the canal entrance lights leading you out into Delaware Bay.

WAYPOINT 20
L 38° 58' 00" N λ 74° 58' 04" W

A capital ship for an ocean trip
Was the "Walloping Window Blind;"
No wind that blew dismayed her crew
Or troubled the captain's mind.
The man at the wheel was made to feel
Contempt for the wildest blo-o-ow,
Tho' it often appeared
When the weather had cleared,
That he'd been in his bunk below.

> "A Capital Ship," Charles Edward Carry

Clearing the canal we set a course about three one zero or three one five degrees magnetic heading for Q G 20ft 5m "19", which would put us right in the channel just below Miah Maull Shoal. We had the whole bay to ourselves, not another vessel in sight and the visibility was great. Al set the sails, putting us in motor sailing mode to gain just a little more drive from the wind. Boy, it was a relief to leave Cape May behind. I don't know what the heck was going on; it sure was different from any other time I have passed through this area. Dark is one thing, but not to be able to see your hand right in front of your face yet see things in the distance clearly is another thing. Oh well, from here on the twilight should brighten into a nice traveling day. Al appearing at the companionway handing me a bagel and egg with coffee sure supported it. In about fourteen hours we should be throwing our lines down at Markley's in Middle River, Maryland. I'm looking forward to an enjoyable time on this part of the run once we get into the main channel and are carried along with the favoring current.

I setting on my perch at the wheel scanning for traffic, pot floats, and other vessels while steering visually towards the intended mark, not having a care in the world, Al was in the companionway where he had a three hundred and sixty degree view of the horizon under the booms and full view of the plotter below. Each time Al popped his head out he had a big smile; he was watching the GPS for speed over ground and our normal speed of six and a half knots was steadily increasing to seven plus, then eight plus. Surely we were in the flood current we wanted to ride on, right on up the Delaware. The real fun was when we reached Elbow of Cross Ledge light and up at the elbow in the channel at mark "32", Al popped out looking over the side checking the marks as we flew by; we're holding nine point nine. Sure enough, we were booking right along, the pedal to the medal; the old *Dragon* had picked up her skirt and was running. The buoys were lying over with the water from the current build up around them on the upstream side and a long tail trailing off the downstream side. Now these are deep-water channel markers, not the usual river or bay sizes. The nice thing about electronic navigation, it is constantly being upgraded so you see right away the change in course, speed, and time to the destination. The old way you would have to know the distance between the marks, time with a stopwatch, then work out the speed using time and distance longhand or with a circular slide rule such as a Time-Speed-Distance-Estimator. Boy, I think of all the times throughout the years Al and I have spent popping in and out of the cabin taking bearings, or timing marks when abeam only to have the information after the fact. The old *Dragon* was in the groove, sails shaped well and drawing, the feel of the wheel and response just the way you want. Out came Al's hand with a couple of cookies and a bigger broader smile.

The Delaware Bay has a bad reputation for fast forming storms and very rough breaking seas along with current of three or more knots. Entering Delaware Bay from the ocean passing between Cape Henlopen and Cape May the deep water favors the south side or Cape Henlopen, which lines you up with the main channel that runs right up the middle of the bay. The big difference in this bay is that on both sides running parallel to the channel are shoals and ledges, some only having three or four feet of water. On the starboard or north east side of the channel is a wide range of depth having from eleven to twenty plus feet of water but a very inconsistent bottom. Although there is sufficient depth for non-ocean-going deep draft vessels, the highs and lows of the bottom create eddies and can cause steep, close breaking seas if wind and current are against each other. This is the area to be in when working up the bay if opposing an ebb current. There's plenty of room for tacking, and the few rivers or holes to divert into are along this shore. Running without a plotter or GPS is not that bad as the lighthouses off to port along the main channel give good references for position. The port or west-southwest side not so, all along the channel are long narrow shoals with depths as low as two feet. Most of the shoreline has shoal water reaching way out from shore, reducing the tacking area to work in with no inlets other then Leipsic River or Bowers Beach, which both could be a bear to enter in foul weather and not that great for an anchorage or finding a slip. If sailing down the bay on a reach or run the west side wouldn't be that challenging, but going up and maybe the chance of losing daylight could turn into a white-knuckle ride. Another factor in causing the building up of rough confused seas is that the Delaware River is long and has a large volume of water always flowing out, and the incoming tide has to push or flow over this. Also, with the ocean's direct approach into the bay the full force of wave surge and wind can sure ruffle the water.

I have had some real good rides up and down the bay on three or four of the Great Ocean Races and on my way to Bermuda on my *Mariah*, a Columbia 28, we sailed down mostly after sunset at hull speed with the boat trying to surf. Another great ride was on the *Good Little Ship*, a full battened gaff rigged cat ketch with bilge boards instead of a centerboard. Sailing on a broad reach, lee board down lee rail awash with the max current all the way up the to the C.&D. The *Dragon* didn't have a good wind off her quarter to drive her lee rail down and put a bone in her teeth, but she sure was enjoying the help of the flood and riding on the backs of the waves. With the increased speed and pressure on the hull the intake of bilge water was minimal, taking a lot of pressure off Al.

As the day grew longer, there were numerous watermen out hauling pots or head boats trolling in and out or around the fishing holes but always out of the channel. This is one place they stay clear of the heavy commercial traffic. With the long straight run, whether inbound or outbound they just travel too fast to take the gamble. Our main concern was the pleasure motor vessels overtaking or opposing, coming in too close, throwing that huge stern wave at us. A stern wave or wake is not a natural wave, as all the energy to make it comes up from below from prop wash in a small concentrated area, making a steep wave. A wave like this does not support the hull as a natural wave does and allows the vessel to drop; this is our main concern with the leakage we have. We just don't know what's going on, whether a plank sprung loose or just caulking worked loose. Luckily we haven't been rocked or thrown around to any great discomfort. The heavy commercial traffic just forms a big long rolling swell, which is easier on the hull, and if from astern we can ride it and get that extra push. There always seems to be traffic way ahead and way astern of us, but when passing they're quite far apart and at a safe distance off. The old *Dragon* just keeps sliding down the rhumb line closing in on the entrance of the Delaware River.

A trip on the Delaware is definitely not a boring one; the lighthouses are interesting in design, what's left of them, and how close the channel is to them - they are right on the edge of the channel. Then the abundance of diversified commercial shipping and pleasure yachts of all sizes, shapes, and conditions keeps you watching and commenting on them. Being part of the Intracoastal Waterway (ICW), it gets its share of transit traffic, especially in the spring and fall. It's fun to try and figure out if the yachts are snowbirds or not by seeing how the decks are covered with fuel cans, life rafts, wind generators, and let's throw in a kayak and a wind- or surf- board for good measure. All of this usually on a hull designed and rigged for performance and the advertisements say you can cruise in it too; speed sells. The Dover Air Force Base is on the south shore, and all types of large aircraft are frequently flying in low for takeoffs or landings. If they come up over your stern and you can't hear them until just overhead and the sound is heard at the same time as the plane passes overhead, it is quite a shock. Ship John Shoal light and the Cohansey River are about where the bay ends and the river starts. It seemed like in no time we had Ship John light abeam and still holding a favorable tide, mild seas, yet still light winds. Al had been watching a group of vessels or a convoy of some sort 'way down the channel slowly gaining on us. Using the binoculars he said it looked like four or more vessels close together and definitely making time on us. We were in a safe area as we could move to starboard off the channel anywhere along this part of the river all the way to the Chesapeake and Delaware Canal (C&D). When closer off our stern, we could see that a tug was towing a dead U.S. naval ship of some sort with two tugs off her stern. Moving to starboard to show we knew they were there and we would stand clear, we then corrected our course to parallel theirs so we could study them. The tug seemed to be working hard as her stern was down and churning up the water, not a rooster tail but definitely prop wash showing she surely had her back into it. The towing hawser was showing the strain as we could visually see it shaking from the strain. All of this with the current, what if she had to tow against the flow! As they got abreast of us it seemed that they slowed to our speed, keeping in the same position. Possibly because the channel at mark "32" has a slight turn to port and to control the towed ship, the tug slowed so that when she turned the ship would be slow enough to have her bow pulled to port and follow the tug's track instead of going in a straight line and overriding the tug. Whatever the reason, it was nice to be able to watch the way they handled the towing of such a big vessel. Now that we were in the river and the channel runs straight for quite a distance before it swings to starboard making a turn around Artificial Island, they might pick up speed before they have to slow down just before the C &D for the swing to port. Then again they could hold this speed all the way up river. Joking, Al said we could call the captain and tell him we were only carrying our lower working sails and could hank on a few more headsails and pull ahead or slow the little Yammy down a few RPMs and pass astern. Hey, if you think our wake will cause you to pitch and roll jerking the hawser, we will back off and just let you pass. It's crazy fun like this that fills in the boring times or rather eliminates the boring times, either way this is the silly shit you talk about when with friends and a round or two of beers is on the table. After all, here was a little thirty-one footer on deck keeping right in stride with the navy's big boys.

  The truth of the matter was we were on the starboard side of the convoy and channel, but to enter the C & D we would have to swing to port either now or later. From here on up to the canal the port side of the channel does not have the area of deep water to work in as the starboard side does and gets skinnier up around Reedy Island and Reedy Bar, plus there is a general anchorage right before the turn into the channel, which would mean more maneuvering. All the while we were moving up the channel and sets of markers were going by, yet we are still abeam of each other. Watching the plotter and knowing the area, we had to have a plan just when to back off on the throttle to pass astern. About this time it seemed they picked up speed and started to pull ahead.

Sure enough the convoy was pulling ahead, maybe that's what all the straining of the tug was about, trying to get more way on now that the channel has a straight run. I'm sure they want to increase speed till they get to the next turn, which will put them well ahead of us. If we don't get antsy and jump the gun, just keep the same speed and course, they should be clear enough for us to move back into the channel astern of them before the C&D. The canal will be our third on this trip but the Chesapeake & Delaware Canal is one of only two commercially vital sea-level canals in the United States. Fourteen miles long, 450 feet wide, and 35 feet deep passing through Delaware and Maryland connecting the Delaware River to the Chesapeake Bay, saving 40 percent of all ship traffic in and out of Baltimore nearly 300 miles. When first opened by the C&D Canal Company in 1829, you entered at Delaware City with locks at Delaware City and St. Georges, Delaware and two at Chesapeake City, Maryland. When taken over by the Federal government in 1919 and designated as the "Intra-coastal Waterway Delaware River to Chesapeake Bay, Delaware and Maryland" and converted to a sea –level operation, the locks were eliminated except the one at Delaware City which is still there but not used. Approaching the entrance to the canal the convoy kept going up river, giving us plenty of clearance behind the tugs to swing to port.

WAYPOINT 21
L 39° 33' 36" N λ 75° 33' 42" W

I've got a mule, her name is Sal,
Fifteen miles on the Erie Canal.
She's a good old worker and a good old pal,
Fifteen miles on the Erie Canal.
"Erie Canal," www.sailorsongs.com

Once inside the breakwater jetties at Reedy Point the water was as flat as glass indicating no air, but watching the water's edge along the rocks you could just about see the current flowing out, meaning that by the time we reached Chesapeake City we would have motored through a slack and now have the current with us. By keeping the same steady pace the old *Dragon* had us right on our predicted time. Being all alone, no traffic coming or going, we held to the middle and the *Dragon* just slid along taking full advantage of the millpond-like surroundings. I don't think many of the yachters realize how technically advanced this system is. Using the state-of-the-art fiber optics, microwave links, television, and radio systems, dispatchers can monitor the full length of the canal.

It was a quiet day, only a few throttle jockeys flying by in their souped up water bugs, picturesque tugs pushing or towing, a few pleasure boats, and one ship overtaking that we had to give way to. The fast motor yachts were up on plane consuming fuel like a drunk at a party and the crew losing the chance to smell the roses. It's great to have the time and desire to leave the rat race behind, to slow down and be in tune with the boat and surrounds. Now only a few houses and the rest of the shoreline is wooded until Chesapeake City. I'm always looking for families or couples fishing along the shore or maybe a glimpse at some wildlife along the way. I highly recommend if you have the time, stop and layover at Chesapeake City. The U.S. Army Corps of Engineers maintains the Canal Museum, which is well worth seeing. There is an anchorage basin but it's shallow, slips are available, and it is a nice town to have dinner in or just mosey around. I think the big attraction at the museum is an 1852 waterwheel measuring 39 feet in diameter, 10 feet wide with 12 troughs which move a 170 tons of water per minute by two 150 horse powered steam engines consuming eight tons of coal daily to transfer the water into the canal. This old system operated continuously through the mid-1920s.

While motoring along taking in all the sights Al handed out a mug of hot coffee, a sandwich, and a piece of fruit followed by some cookies. This is the life; all of our movement is straight down the rhumb line, beautiful sunny day, right on time with the current, not a care in the world. Once out of the canal we will be in the Elk River, whose channel is as narrow as the canal giving the water hydrostatic pressure so it really increases speed and makes the buoys look as though they are swimming upstream. Clearing the Elk River we will enter the headwaters of the Chesapeake Bay, which is my backyard or playground and living here gives me bragging rights. I feel the same as Al Roper wrote in the chanty "A Ballad of Captain Briggs" -

> He dreams of crystal waters
>   And crabs and fish galore
> And not a trace of garbage
>   To wash upon the shore
> He loves the bays and rivers
>   He knows the tides and winds
> When you sail with Captain Briggs, my boys,
>   Everybody wins.

First, the Chesapeake Bay qualifies as an estuary because it is a semi-enclosed coastal body of water whose salinity gradient is measurable from its freshwater drainage to the ocean entrance. Second, it is the largest bay in the United States (2,500 square miles), the longest (195 miles), has the most tributaries (150) and a shoreline longer then the entire West Coast (4,000 miles). Third, another difference from other bays is the Bay's length is just right for a semi-diurnal tidal pattern, giving it a twice daily tide; if the middle of the Bay has a high tide the two ends, Capes Henry and Charles at the mouth, and the Elk and Susquehanna Rivers at the headwaters, are having low tide at the same time. If numbers impress you, the bay holds 18 trillion gallons of water, needing from its tributaries an average of 70,000 cubic feet of water flowing into the bay every second. In 1986 the seafood harvest was more than 200 million pounds with an annual dockside value exceeding $100 million. What does all this mean to a loose-footed vagabond sailor? Well, with all that shoreline and tributaries there sure must be some good hurricane holes or just gunkholing spots to set an anchor in. Producing that much seafood, it seems a man could live off the land chicken necking for blue crabs or wetting a line to bring aboard some fine fish for dinner. With all this commercial seafood harvesting, the workboats and marinas would sure be interesting, you could have work done if needed or, heavens forbid, find work. The fishing ports will keep you interested in the systems for commercially handling of blue crabbing from hard to soft-shell, oyster and soft-shell clam harvesting to shipping while waiting out the weather if you are holed up. In home waters like this, I sail by the seat of my pants free of the plotter and charts, just read the water, watch the sky, and pay attention to traffic and marks that seem to be in a straight line.

 The wind is up some now that we are in the river, but not enough to sail on if we want to be in before sundown. Al had figured we would get east or southeast winds when on the

Bay and they would build as the day grew. With the leak still on his mind and knowing how the Bay can kick up a sea with its steep chop, his concern was if we had to head into it and pound for any distance we could do some harm. Up here in the Elk River we were between high banks and really out of the wind, but when we clear Turkey Point I like to leave the channel, which makes more easterly down to Grove Point on the north shore of the Sassafras River. The channel crosses the mouth of the river close to Howell Point on the south shore, then runs the rest of the way under the lee of a high shoreline keeping the seas down. If you go straight down the bay from Turkey Point like I do, you are out in the middle in open water. I told Al that we didn't have to worry till we got to Worton Point, then the run from there to Poole's Island would get rough as a corn cob if the wind did build as predicted. But we have a couple good anchorages to duck into if we have to lay up; one even has a Coast Guard Station.

WAYPOINT 22
L 39° 24' 35" N λ 76° 02' 08" W

The fair breeze blew, the white foam flew,
The furrow followed free;
We were the first that ever burst
Into that silent sea.
> *Rime of the Ancient Mariner*, Samuel T. Coleridge

Sure enough, staying in the channel running along the shore below Howell Point in the lee the seas were down, but to the west out in the open bay whitecaps were making the waves look like snow-capped frozen furrows of a plowed field on a winter's day. As we approached Worton Point we could see out past the wind shadow of the point and sure enough, it's going to be like riding in a Model T Ford over those frozen furrows-like waves to Poole's Island. Surely not as bad as when we came out of the Cape Cod Canal into Buzzards Bay, it was dead on the bow. We will have it off the quarter and beam, but after rounding the island we will have a quartering or following sea all the way to Middle River. Then going up Middle River it will be in sheltered waters clear to Markley's Marina. Now this is my stomping grounds and I would love to lay the Yammie to rest and have a good sail if it were not for the worry of the leak. I know Al's concerned, and at this steady pace we won't be in till at least four o'clock, shop quitting time. We have to make arrangements for a slip and maybe for a haul out tomorrow to check the bottom. The sipping pump has been coming on regular but not at an alarming rate. There's a big difference between owner and crew: I know the marina, the work they do, and who to have do it, but to Al the boat is far from home, the extent of work that might be needed is unknown, and he has no personal contacts to deal with. The leak is real, she's got some age on her, and it takes an old-time craftsman to understand her needs and the correct way to go about fixing her. Add the unknown amount of time needed, distance to travel, and God only knows cost, before the *Dragon* can spit fire in defiance again. This is a lot on anyone's mind. It makes the seas look bigger, the wind feel stronger, the distance to go longer, and you feel that time is not on your side. What is it they say, 'been there, done that?' I went to Bermuda on my twenty-eight foot Columbia sloop barefooted and on a shoestring, you think I wasn't cutting it close? Concerned? Be in the Gulf Stream in a northeaster reefed down to a handkerchief, riding through mountain size breaking seas and the wife who has never flown before is in Bermuda alone waiting for you.

The average depth on the bay is twenty-one feet and that's about the depth we'll be running in, but as we approach Poole's Island there's a string of shoals with some places seven to eleven feet. With the wind out of Worton Creek the fetch can build up a good sea only to pile up on the shoals and build up bigger seas. Oh, the *Dragon* has no trouble at all handling this type of sea, she's sailed this Bay in all kinds of weather and anything the Bay can throw at her. She's won her share of Great Chesapeake Bay Schooner Races and most if not all in winds thirty and plus, real gear busting conditions. As we moved out into the open water, the stern would go down into the trough and you could hear the exhaust underwater, then the wave would roll on picking up the stern and trying to shove her along. This is not a trochoidal wave, as waves on the Bay never reach the twenty feet from peak to peak, which a thirty-footer with a twenty-foot waterline needs. The old timers learned how to design these hulls and get the most out of them on multi sea conditions. A true trochoidal wave moving at the same speed as the boat supports the bow and stern at the same time. Now the *Dragon* is not pounding or laboring or working the standing rigging, putting a strain on the hull. But I could see Al's concern and the amount of attention he was giving the bilge. Al, just before we reach the end of the island there's a hole about forty-one feet deep right up against a ten foot ledge and it makes the trough like falling into a hole, it's only about four or five boat lengths but rough. After that we can fall off some and start to round the island, then we'll have a following sea, start the sheets, and settle into a run.

Heading up Middle River while the *Dragon* was under the command of the autopilot we dropped the sails, had them furled, gaskets on, and had just finished putting on the sail covers when I realized we were standing off the end of Markley's pier. I pointed ashore and told Al, take her in to the travel lift slip, and on the port you will see a long finger pier where we can lay. Lines down, springs set, electric plugged in for the pump, the *Dragon* was secured and the crew ready for shore leave. It's been a long haul from City Island, New York, and that continuous worry about the amount of leakage. Eight bells or four o'clock yard time, we were right on our predicted time of arrival. For me I was home back in the boatyard that I have had a boat in since nineteen sixty-nine and where I work when at home, end of my plot. For the *Dragon* it is just a waypoint along the trip.

The whole shop crew and their friends plus a couple of watermen were sitting around or leaning on their pickups drawing on Bud Light long necks. The beer's over in the cooler, you ready to go back to work? Hell no, just passing through, got a leak to check out, some varnishing to get done, and then off to the race. Hey, Jeff, we put the boat on the finger pier next to Mike's, okay? Hell no, that's for paying customers. Well, if you haul her tomorrow she won't be there.

WAYPOINT 23
L 39° 18' 41" N   λ 76° 25' 48" W

Grab your nets,
And get on the boat
Just feel the waves abumpin'
There's a big ole full moon
Out tonight
And we're all going crab hunting.
Yea, we're all going crab hunting.
>"Crab Hunting", Bruce Myers,
>*Stinkpot & Rags*

What the hell is wrong now besides being a sailboat? We really don't know but we've been pumping water ever since Cape May. When did you leave there, two days ago? Hey, it only took fourteen hours and about ten gallons of fuel. Fourteen hours, what you do, row? Poor Al just stood there with a beer in his hand knowing that I was the only blow boater in the crowd and the oldest has-been and receptacle of all the jollification. He knew this surely was not the time to make arrangements for the haul out, these guys had done a day's work and the yard was shut down so let it lay.

We spent the night in my apartment at the "funny farm" (Oak Crest Retirement Community) but made sure that we were back in the yard before eight so we could dust the hull with the sawdust before haul-out in hopes of finding the leak. Our goal was to be hauled out right after the shop had their eight-thirty coffee break. Markley's is an old family-owned yard and has a very laid-back management approach. Explain the best you can of what you feel is wrong, or tell them your needs. But you better realize if a workboat comes in needing repairs, he definitely will be worked on ahead of you so he can go back to work. That's one thing old Captain Ben set in place from the very beginning.

In nineteen forty-five, Captain Ben Markley filled in an old marsh to reclaim some of his waterfront property, added a railway, hung a sign Markley's Inc., and was in business. At first, it was kind of a part-time operation as Captain Ben was a full time captain for the Glenn L. Martin Co., towing seaplanes around the river and even on the Bay at times. Everything was low key and basically hand built, a true blue collar working man's marina. Most of the customers were friends or local watermen who did their own work. This was in the days before travel-lifts that give you the ability to move boats around on shore so several boats can be worked on at a time. At first there was no railway winch to haul up the cradle and boat. In order to haul out he would secure the *Bucky*, his workboat, to a block and tackle attached to a block at the head of the railway, then to the cradle. Then he would run *Bucky* out from the railway, hauling the cradle and boat up. If more than one boat was to be worked on, it had to be rolled sideways off the cradle onto timbers lying at right angles to the railway, last hauled, first put back over.

Young Ben, one of the sons, was involved in all kinds of boat repair and had built a couple of small boats on his own while still in school. Out of school and out in the working world he went to work at the Sparrows Point Shipyard doing wood work on ships. Then he took a job at the Owens Yacht Co. on the assembly line making different parts for new yachts. All of these jobs were short-lived but good training and an eye opener. Realizing the potential of the yard, he put all his effort into developing the yard into a first-rate boat yard. Tackling all types of repair jobs and keeping the commercial watermen's boats in service proved that Markley's could handle anything. As business grew so did the yard, it was one of the very first yards to have a travel lift, then a building large enough to drive the lift into. Now the yard has a 60 ton and a 30 ton lift and a second shop that can hold two 46 footers.

Knowing the Bay's wave patterns and what the watermen liked and wanted in a workboat, Ben designed and built a 28-footer for crabbing or fishing. The watermen liked them but said the market was good and they could really use bigger boats. So a 46 footer or 42 footer out of the same mold was produced, next a 35 was made when the market got softer. Many old yacht hulls have come in, been cut down, re-powered, and workboat type cabins installed so they could go back out as commercial vessels. The largest, a 50-foot sport fisherman that has been to Costa Rica and back in pursuit of billfish, proves the durability of a Markley. This is a modern powerboat boat yard, all fiberglass construction; the woodpile here is only food for the fire eating dragon better known as the big wood stove. The yard still services a couple of old wood deadrisers but take care, *Green Dragon*!

Every morning Miss Conney, young Captain Ben's widow, brings in fresh baked buns or cake for the coffee break. Sure enough right after the coffee break Jeffery, the third generation Markley, came over to us; I thought you wanted to be hauled this morning? We do, well, I can't till you get her in the slip. Do you want to chock her up here or will she be out for a while? If it's ok I'd like to see what's wrong first, ok no trouble I don't need the lift, you got time to do what you need. I saw the relief on Al's face when he realized Jeff was just jerking my chain and we were about to get the show on the road. As Jeffery lowered her down on some chocks, Al noticed a lot more water coming out between the ballast and keel than he could remember. The first thought was that a keel bolt was leaking; in the past he had had Crockers replace some. We had checked this area in the bilge back in Cape May and had seen no signs of leakage. Bilge water would not have flowed out that fast and not in such a large area as Al had said. Water coming out of a leak only has gravity moving it, but when in the water the displacement of the boat is pushing the water in. Looking at the keel with Al, I just didn't feel this was the leak. We had pumped her dry before leaving her for the night and she was dry when hauled. If the keel bolts leaked that bad, they would have sunk us for sure. I in turn was looking for seams with sawdust sucked into them indicating a leak. No luck, the bottom was smooth and none of the caulking was pinched or showing signs of being pulled out, and she surely didn't have nail rot. But the seam at the stern above the water line where the planking and transom joined had quite a gap. Again she was dry when we boarded this morning and still dry when hauled. I just think the water Al saw at the keel was trapped between the keel and ballast and Al had never noticed it before this haul out. Besides, it had already stopped. Up forward in the forefoot area none of the seams appeared to be open or having plank movement. In Cape May we saw what appeared to be water coming in around the deadwood but could not be sure because of the lead ballast placed there.

It seemed that she didn't leak, or very little at the most, when not underway. Because of the re-powering, the prop pitch and size had been enlarged and the shaft torque increased. This would definitely pull the stern down and generate a lot more water pressure on the underbody of the stern. One thing for sure, water was coming from the lazarette area and moreso when underway.

Now down here in Bay country we use roof caulking in the seams - cheap, it sticks to anything, stays pliable, can be painted over, but can be easily raked out if seams are to be repayed. If it was good enough through all these years for all the wooden yachts, skipjacks buyboats, and deadraises, it was surely good enough for my *Mary G*... I would not recommend something for the *Dragon* that I would not use on my own boat. Al is used to using the new caulking compounds such as Polyseamseal or Life-Calk and reluctantly said ok. Roof caulking only comes in black so I only caulked the underside of the painted hull where it didn't show and below the water line. If the transom was the area of the leak, then it should be raked out and be recaulked with cotton or oakum and repayed.

She didn't leak when she re-entered the water, but we won't find out till we work the hull either sailing or powering. Once back in the water Al contracted Jeffery's brother, Little Benny, to strip and varnish the cap rail. Knowing it would take a couple of days, we started to remove all the things from the boat that weren't needed for the race such as the inflatable dink, dink motor, and gas can. The more you look around, the more you see that has to be rearranged to make room for the new crew that will come aboard for the race. Checking the standing and running rigging you always find lines that need whipping, replacing, or rerunning. When she docks at Fells Point in Baltimore we'll want to socialize and take in all the pre-race activities, so this is the place to do all the preparing and maintenance.

Working and hanging out in a boatyard is not all that bad. Here there are a lot of different things going on. One section of the yard is for crab boats, and every afternoon they come in off the Bay, turn around out at the far end of the piers, and back down about four hundred feet to their slip. Never a change in speed or course, they handle them the same every day, windy, with or without current, no fuss or bother. Bushels of crabs are offloaded to their trucks, a wash down, next day's bait sent aboard, all in the same motion, no fuss or bother. Elsewhere in the yard there are probably two or three major repair jobs in different stages going on. Then there's Duke. If ever there was a boatyard dog like a junkyard dog Duke is the boatyard dog of dogs. A full tailed boxer with full floppy ears (one has a good size piece bite out by a wild hog but Duke got the better end - it was the end for the hog) and enough scars on his face to back off a truck driver. He lives out on the schooner and has full run of the yard all day. But he has to know where every worker is and wants to oversee his work. In the winter he has his own rug by each wood stove. The trouble is, if at one he can't see the other men in the other shop, so that keeps him going back and forth. At lunchtime when we blow the dust and dirt off ourselves, he stands in line for his turn and he needs it as much as we do. When John, his rightful owner, travels he used to put him in doggy day care, but he has been thrown out of three and asked not to come back by others. Not a place for a seasoned schooner dog. When we arrived at the yard, he saw me and I got the greeting he gives me every morning when the day starts, and the whole time in the yard he kept tabs on my movements.

When aboard the *Dragon* you are never bored, someone is always coming up to the boat asking where she's from, who built her, how old, how long have you had her, where is she off to? She's a head turner. Many remember that her first arrival was by truck and knew she was here for the race to defend her first in her class, When traveling, a good part of the pleasure, especially in a classic like the *Dragon*, is the people you meet and the stories about their boats and ports of call that they've been in. It sure whets your appetite to follow in their wake for the experience and to see for yourself. Even though this is a powerboat yard, about sixty percent of the boats here are sail. There's a fifty-two foot staysail schooner the *Edlyn Rose* (Duke's home) which will also participate in the race. Then there's an older wooden ketch along with these new-fangled glass ketches, yawls, and sloops. Many of the boats are set up for serious racing and win their fair share of trophies. With a cross section of boats like this, you're sure going to meet some interesting sailors. But the hot shots on the Tupperware boats just can't figure out why we need all that running rigging and no winches and why gaffs and overhanging booms. When we tell them we fly two spinners at once with no penalty they just look at you with that blank stare; yes, we are different.

WAYPOINT 24
L 39° 16' 34" N λ 76° 34' 64" W

> The maestro of all revelry
>   He parties with the best
> He charms the pretty ladies
>   And teases all the rest
> Regattas, beer and oysters –
>   Then do it all again!
> When you play with Captain Briggs, my boys,
>   Everybody wins.
>
>   Al Roper, *The Great Chesapeake Bay Schooner Race Chanty Song Book*

    Thank God there is a time when all the work is done and the *Dragon* is in Bristol fashion sporting her new-varnished rails and neatly whipped rope ends and appears to have a dry bilge. We made good time on the projects, had a good time, and now it's our departure time.

    Taking in the lines, swinging the bow seaward working our way out along the pier for the river was the beginning of the end. In about thirty-five nautical miles we will be in Fells Point Baltimore, the end of the journey for me but the location of the start of the Great Chesapeake Bay Schooner Race that was the sole reason for the *Dragon* to come south. She's a classic boat regatta race junky and thinks nothing of tramp sailing from Maine to Virginia to be on the starting line. Not much air for the distance we have to travel, so under our usual double-reefed main and the steady push of the Yanmar, we were on our way. Sure enough, the same old stream of water coming from the lazarette area, damn, not what you want to see anytime, far less before a hundred-plus mile race. On the way to Broadway Pier at Fells Point, we stopped to top off the fuel tank. While made fast to the fuel dock I asked Al to put her in gear and gave her some throttle. A-ha, it is the prop wash! It's forcing water in at the horn timber or seam between the planking and transom. No big deal right now. To fix it right will mean raking out the seams, checking for rot and loose fastenings, which I don't think is an issue. This would mean a time consuming haul out on the hard, which we don't have time for. As far as the race is concerned, you can't run the engine anyway so she won't leak, not much anyway. This was still a big concern for Al and he was weighing all his options, should she be hauled out again, take the chance and race, or start to make arrangements for a complete repair. On the lighter side, Al noticed that the fuel pump had a large sign on it advertising beer right under the heading to Fill Up. Out came the camera and he had me hold the fuel hose as though I was drinking from it, only in Baltimore. One thing for sure, a true sailor can be under the stress of dark clouds but can find humor in the simplest thing.

    The Great Chesapeake Bay Schooner Race is the crown jewel of all schooner events. This event draws forty or more schooners, making it the largest schooner agglomeration in the world, drawing vessels from all corners of the chart. Such as the *Tole Mour* a 156 ft. three-master which after returning from Hawaii signed up, then returned for two more races. Other vessels as far away as Lunenburg, Nova Scotia such as the 181 ft. Grand Banks fishing schooner *Bluenose II* have participated. One, the *Tree Of Life,* a 93-footer, was on a six-year circumnavigation when she heard about the race while cruising New England waters, called to register, and still sends best wishes from wherever she is. Size has nothing to do with who shows up, every size down to the *Tom Swifts*, a 16.7 footer, and every type of construction from ferroconcrete, aluminum, iron, (1885 *Pioneer*, the first iron sloop built in the United States) to good old-fashioned wood construction. *Martha White,* a 65 footer built on the lines of *Bluenose II* by Earle Williams's using old style construction and 200-year-old long-leaf yellow pine for the ribs and planks, and 4000 locust trunnels using 8000 blind wedges.

If you are a schooner nut and have been bit by the schooner bug, this is one event you don't want to miss. This is no regatta, trade show, and surely no boat show, but they sure show off their stuff when mustered together. This is the chance to find friends you only see at the race or others that seem to attend all the schooner events. Here is a collection of boats built back in the day when the architect designed the hardware as well as the boat and the boatyard cast them in silicone bronze. No cookie cutter plastic hardware here. All schooners are rigged the same way, but each has a different way of going about it and a good deck hand can figure it out, so here is a chance to get some new ideas. A true classic has no winches: everything is moved, hauled, or secured by block and tackle with muscle power. Little tricks on mechanical advantage or other systems of running rigging can be picked up. Here is the chance to see some great wood work and little tricks that might come in handy. When below you see how someone has made more efficient use of space and peek to see if your competitor has stripped her out to lighten her for the race. Talking to other crewmembers and owners you get the true opinions of marine products and the way they did things, not like when talking to a salesman who is building a paycheck. One tour of the *Green Dragon* and you see the real advantages of the changes Al has done throughout the years. I think unconsciously Al had done this through the years of boat-hopping and sailing on different types of craft. Removing the tiller and installing the wheel, the skylight in the saloon, and without a doubt the compact installation of the Yanmar. For sure, he is a walking marine encyclopedia and is taken seriously. If new to the game or not signed on to any boat, you can walk the docks, as they say, as though you are looking for a job but instead only looking for a berth for the race.

WAYPOINT 25
L 39° 16' 31" N λ 76° 35' 35" W

Fiddler's Green: A sailor's paradise, where public houses, dance halls, and other similar amusements are plentiful and the ladies are accommodating. It really had only a celestial and not a terrestrial connotation in the sailor's mind, a sort of permanent sensual Elysium or sailor's heaven but still vaguely related to the delights enjoyed by sailors ashore with money in their pockets.

-The Oxford Companion to Ships and the Sea

The run from the fuel dock to Broadway Pier in Fells Point is a short distance so the main was not set but fenders, spring and dock lines were laid out in preparation for making up to another vessel or wherever the dockmaster assigns us. Motoring past Henderson's piers we looked to see if any of the big boys such as the *Lettie G. Howard* were berthed yet. As we came alongside Belts Wharf, we could see the forest of masts above the buildings, indicating a good turnout. Not knowing our docking arrangements we came in view of the foot of Broadway, the entrance to Fells Point. There made up to the bulkhead at Browns Wharf as though a sentry at the gates of Fiddler's Green was the *Norfolk Rebel,* now this is where we want to raft up if asked. Sure enough when Steve Briggs saw us, we were given the high sign to come alongside. These two boats are berth buddies at Rebel Marine, the home of the *Norfolk Rebel; Dragon* will winter in Norfolk after the race. If Captain Lane Briggs were still alive, he would have asked us to come aboard for a spot of tea. Never invite a man for rum in public - a man's choice of drink is his business and a sailor's image has to be held high.

Captain Lane of the *Norfolk Rebel* had commissioned Merritt Walter to design a sail-assisted workboat for the fishing trade, as well as for towing and salvage work. From the very beginning, it was a tongue-in-cheek operation. As Jim Heely of the Tanner's Creek Whalers wrote in the sea chanty *The Norfolk Rebel,*

> When the keel was laid the doubters said "you're just an April Fool"
>
> Your ideas are impractical! You're breaking all the rules
>
> But the lubbers who could not believe in a boat they'd never seen,
>
> Are the ones who are left behind by the Tugantine.

Gas was at an all time shortage, causing long lines at gas stations as well as preventing people from traveling or moving about as they wanted to. In response, the government was offering grants to help develop systems to conserve fuel. A sail–assisted tug could harness the power of the wind to get that added knot or two when in harness at work or while under sail only when in transit. From the drawing board came the off-sets and scantling for a stout Tugantine with a high almost plumb stem and a shear angle sweeping down to just about the raised deck area under the wheelhouse, then dropping down to the after working deck. Just forward of amidships the wheelhouse set on a raised deck area. Foredeck large enough for a fish hole under, afterdeck large enough for towing bite and enough space to flake down the towing hawser. To give her the power for tugging she is powered by a 320 hp. Detroit 8v71 throwing a 44x40 four blade prop. She is rigged as a baldheaded gaff schooner with a yardarm for a square sail that can be sent aloft from deck, making her look salty and traditional. A vee-shaped tubular bowsprit or widow maker can be hauled within the hull under the foredeck while in pushing gear when made up to a barge. Black hull and spars and red trim on the bow to the white wheelhouse make her stand out but business like. Being a rebel, she sports a pair of black powder swivel cannons on port and starboard rails of the bridge deck, plus in the galley there is a draft beer tap on the forward bulkhead (removed after 9/11). She is a rebel in spirit, no conformist and definitely not racial.

Moored at the entrance to Fells Point she sets in perfectly, she represents everything the Point is, a true blue collar worker, she's a schooner as much as the first fast clippers and trading schooners built here, a design as crude as the cobblestones and the 17th century buildings. The *Rebel* is also the catalyst of the Great Chesapeake Bay Schooner Race. After working at towing, fishing, and salvaging, Capt. Lane started escorting tall ships participating in *OpSail* festivities. For whatever reason, Capt. Lane challenged the then brand new *Pride of Baltimore ll* to race from Baltimore to Norfolk as the old time cargo-hauling schooners did. The challenge was, first across the finish line got the prize of a bottle of beer. Schooners were the workhorses of the day plying up and down the Bay as the tractor-trailer of today does on I-95. The fastest schooner garnered the highest price by outdoing her competition. To bring this working ethic full circle, a gift from the Mayor of Norfolk was sailed up to the Mayor of Baltimore as cargo. Word got out about the challenge and whetted other schooner captains' appetite to join in on the fun, not knowing that they were the railway that launched the Great Chesapeake Bay Schooner Race. Town Point Yacht Club members got caught up in the challenge and sailed north in company with the *Rebel*.

After arriving, they were told that the *Pride* was out on a good will trip and had to forfeit, so the challenge was put off till the next year – but not the race. Hurricane warnings, with southerlies, did not hold back the schooners *Flutterby, Patricia Divine, American Rover, Bonnie Rover, Clipper City,* and of course *Norfolk Rebel* from carrying out their mission, and off down the Bay on the first race. First grew the gathering, which became a race, then the race became "Racing to Save the Bay," a race on a mission. With the work of hundreds of volunteers and community supporters, the race has raised over $130,000 for the educational endeavors of the Chesapeake Bay Foundation.

The captain realized that most of the charter schooners working in New England have to pass through the Chesapeake going to southern ports to winter. He knew that the crews were always in the public's eye when chartering, with no time for them to pal around with each other or be able to locate a new berth if their ship was being laid up for the season. If the schooners stopped off in Fells Point and laid over a day or so with no charters, the crews could intermingle, relax, and party. Then they all could take off and race on down the Bay. No one ever thought that so many schooners would show up and enjoy the layover. At all of the ports of call throughout the summer season, word spread throughout the fleet. Each year more and more schooners showed up, and now the private-owned fleet of schooner yachts has filled in the void left by the corporate-owned charter schooners that can't participate because of economics.

The real enjoyment of the race is this is one time schoonermen can be in the company of so many diversified schooners in all kinds of sailing conditions. The whole fleet leaves Baltimore harbor and speeds down to the mouth of the Severn River off Annapolis for the start of the 127 nm race to Thimble Shoal Light off Norfolk, Virginia. There are two finishes, first for Class B & C eighty nautical miles down the rhumb line, then Class AA and A at Thimble Shoal. If Class B and C keep racing to Thimble Shoal, the one with the best corrected time wins bragging rights. During the whole race you are in company with other schooners night and day, crossing tacks, being overtaken or overtaking someone. Most of the races have started in dead calms or light following winds, only to have a cold front come through with gear-breaking, sail destroying fifty mph plus winds. With light air starts and such a range of winds, you can see just about every sail made or tried on a schooner. Gaff topsails on fore and main, fisherman's, flying jibs, inner and outer jibs, topmast staysails, and gollywobblers can and will be flown. Yes, they even fly two spinnakers at the same time; if they could, they'd set a moonraker. During all of this, as in any race, you're constantly trying to keep tabs on your competition and how much sail she has pressed on. Ratings do not change because of added sail area aloft, so a lot of top hamper is carried. When crossing the Patuxent or Potomac Rivers, exposed areas in the mouth of the rivers is no place to be when the front hits you if over-canvassed. Worse yet, it is after a wild sail through the night making multiple sail changes only to be setting in a dead calm at daybreak, then watching astern on the horizon the fleet you had overtaken slowly gaining on you. New wind, but do they have to be on the leading edge?

    This is what brought Al and the *Dragon*: a chance to participate and take it all in while partying in a real Fiddler's Green. For me, this is the end of the line, time to pack my bag and sign off the *Green Dragon*, walk the pier, and find *Pirate's Lady* and sign on for the Race.

> The sails are furled, our work is done,
> Leave her, Johnny, leave her!
> And now on shore we'll have our fun.
> It's time for us to leave her!
>
> *The Great Chesapeake Bay Schooner Race
> Chanty Song Book*

Acknowledgements

While writing this tale and looking back I realized how many people had such an important impact in the course of my life and my being accepted in the world of sailing. Without this start I would not have been able to tell such a tale or meet so many interesting people. First was Dr. Richard Von Rigler who introduced me to sailing and allowed me to use his twenty foot sloop *Little Lady*, then his fifty two foot schooner the *Variant* at will. This was the beginning of my love affair with traditional boats and the old ways of the trade. Elizabeth Dunbar stood her watch through all the rough times and put up with my bad spelling and mispronunciation of words, not to mention having to learn and double check the proper use of old sea terms to make this tale come to life. For the cover Mr. Larry LeGault graciously granted permission to use his photo of the *Green Dragon* laying on her mooring in Spruce Head Maine. Joining the crew to bring her magic touch with graphics, Patricia Beauchamp worked with Elizabeth Dunbar to create the cover I had envisioned. Thanks to Allan Bezanson for his friendship and invitation to crew on the *Green Dragon*, then for taking me in tow to hobnob with him and his friends. Along the trip we met people like Mr. Mudd Sharrigan, who took the time to invite us to his home and in great detail showed us how a sailor's knife is made and the proper use and care of it. Thanks to Mr. Rick Thorpe of Harborfields Housekeeping Cottages for the invitation to spend time with him and his other guests, and all of the people at City Island N.Y. and Markley's Marina, Inc. who treated us as close friends providing us with great memories.

Author Jay Irwin

The wife and I learned to sail on Doctor Richard Von Rigler's sloop *Little Lady* and were offered the full use of his boat if I would manage and do the work needed on the boat. Five years later Doc bought the schooner *Variant,* and with the same arrangement the wife and I sailed her for five years. During this time I was taking United States Power Squadron courses from Basic Boating to Celestial Navigation. Having to take care of Doc's boats I was learning every aspect of boat maintenance and handling. Doc sold the *Variant*, so off I went looking for my own boat and from a friend I found out about one that was cheap but needed work. Now the proud owner of the *Mary G.*, a 31 foot sloop named after my wife, we cast us off on our own. The old girl needed some work, really it had to be completely rebuilt, but it was not considered as work. The wife and I would only work on her during the winter, then the whole family would sail and enjoy her all summer. We started cruising the Bay and joined the Glenmar Sailing Association. This got me into round the buoy racing, long distance racing, then off shore. In August of 'sixty nine I bought my new 28 foot Columbia sloop *Mariah* and was off the following May the thirtieth to Bermuda with the Navigation class. All of this led to delivery work up and down the East coast and bringing boats home from the Caribbean or Bermuda. Then the Great Chesapeake Bay Schooner Race started and I got the chance to ship as crew and hang out with schooner men. First was the *Marilyn*, then *Farewell*, *Ocean Star, Lettie G. Howard, Pirate's Lady, Virginia,* and *Quintessence.*

> One road leads to London
> One road leads to Wales
> My road leads me seaward
> To white dripping sails
>
> "Roadways," John Masefield

Owner-Skipper Al Bezanson

Allan Bezanson grew up with Farmall tractors and two dozen dairy cows in Northborough, Massachusetts, went on to Northeastern for a BS in Mechanical Engineering, and forsaking earlier interests in farm machinery and stock car racing, took up with flying machines at the Naval Air Test Center. In 1960, in accord with a plan hatched five years earlier, he departed from his job as a Carrier Suitability Flight Test Engineer to sail a 26 foot Monomoy Surf Boat from Boston to the British Virgin Islands and back with two college classmates. *Serendipity* had been converted to an able ketch by his friend Walter Ramsden. It was Walter who introduced Allan to sailing in an Indian Class racing sloop during his college years. The ten-month *Serendipity* cruise thoroughly depleted the financial resources of the three. It had cost each of them $5/day. But in those days engineering jobs were plentiful and within a month of his return to Boston Allan was on Ascension Island working as an Airborne Test Conductor in an ICBM program.

By 1962 the financial picture improved thanks to a flying bonus, and a search was underway for a more substantial vessel. And so the schooner *Brenda Lee* came into the picture. She was discovered on a mooring right off the end of a Logan Airport runway. *Brenda Lee,* or *Lady Millie* in her early life, became *Green Dragon,* and at 33 feet, 6 net tons she seemed more than ample compared with little *Serendipity*. At the time Allan had a vision of heading off again to the islands, but in the same year a better plan evolved, for he had met an artist named Phyllis, right there on Long Wharf where both lived, and in 1963 they were married on the schooner, under sail, and had soon settled in Gloucester where a daughter and son joined the crew. By this time work with fish processing equipment was (and still is) supporting the Bezansons and providing for the care and feeding of *Green Dragon*.

In Allan's words, "When I first met Jay in Baltimore in 1997 I was impressed with his photographic memory, but had I known he would set down on paper some of the things I said (and may have repeated) during the many miles we sailed together I perhaps would have been more careful in the telling. If this story is published I will be reading it for the first time but have no doubt Jay's account will match some version of what he had been told. Unless, that is, his story was designed as some form of retribution for having to endure the skipper's company, the menu, and the not-so-tight decks on *Green Dragon*. In any case he has been a great friend and the finest kind of shipmate."

References

American Sail Training Association. *Sail Tall Ships! A Directory of Sail Training & Adventure at Sea.* 15th ed., Lori A. Aguiar, ed. Providence: 2003

[The] American College Dictionary. Barnhart, Clarence L., ed in chief. New York: Random House, 1954

Burnham Brothers Railway: Stories from the Neighborhood. An Oral History. Ann Nichols & Harriet Webster, eds. Gloucester: Gloucester Maritime Heritage Center, n.d.

Chapman, C. F. *Piloting, Seamanship and Small Boat Handling.* 51st ed. New York: Hearst, 1974

Colcord, Joanna Carver. *Sea Language Comes Ashore.* Cambridge: Cornell Maritime Press, 1945

Davis, Charles G. *How Sails are made and handled: with a chapter on racing links.* Reprint. First published New York: Rudder Publishing Co., 1922

Encyclopedia of Sailing, Yacht Racing / Cruising. Robert Schnarff and Richard Henderson. New York: Harper & Row, 1971

Farson, Robert H. *The Cape Cod Canal*, 2nd ed. Yarmouth Port: Cape Cod Historical Publications, 1993

The Great Chesapeake Bay Schooner Race Chanty Song Book

Isil, Olivia A. *When a Loose Cannon Flogs a Dead Horse There's the Devil to Pay.* Camden: International Marine, 1996

[The] Oxford Companion to Ships & the Sea. Peter Kemp, ed. London: Oxford, 1976

Mackinnon, A. J. *The Unlikely Voyage of Jack de Crow.* Woodbridge, Suffolk: Seafarer Books, 2002

Rosbe, Judith Westlund. *Images of America: The Beverly Yacht Club.* Charleston, SC: Arcadia, 2006

Royce, Patrick M. *Royce's Sailing Illustrated.* Marina del Rey: Western Marine Enterprises, 1988

Schult, Joachim R. *The Sailing Dictionary.* Translated & revised by Barbara Webb. London: Adlard Coles Ltd., 1981

Van Gaasbeck, Richard M. *A Practical Course in Wooden Boat and Ship Building.* Chicago: Frederick J. Drake, 1919

WoodenBoat Magazine. WoodenBoat Publications, Inc., www.woodenboat.com

www.sailorsongs.com

Yankees Under Sail. Richard Heckman, ed. Dublin NH: Yankee, Inc., 1968